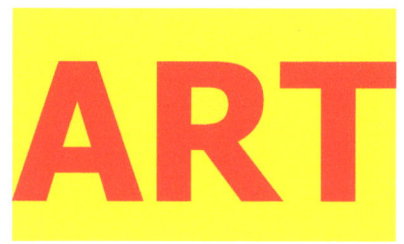

ECKHARD SCHMITTNER

& & &

BETTINA BAUCH

IMPRESSUM

Eckhard Schmittner & Bettina Bauch
© 2018, Eckhard Schmittner & Bettina Bauch
Alle Rechte vorbehalten.
Coverbild: Eckhard Schmittner &Bettina Bauch
Covergestaltung: Eckhard Schmittner

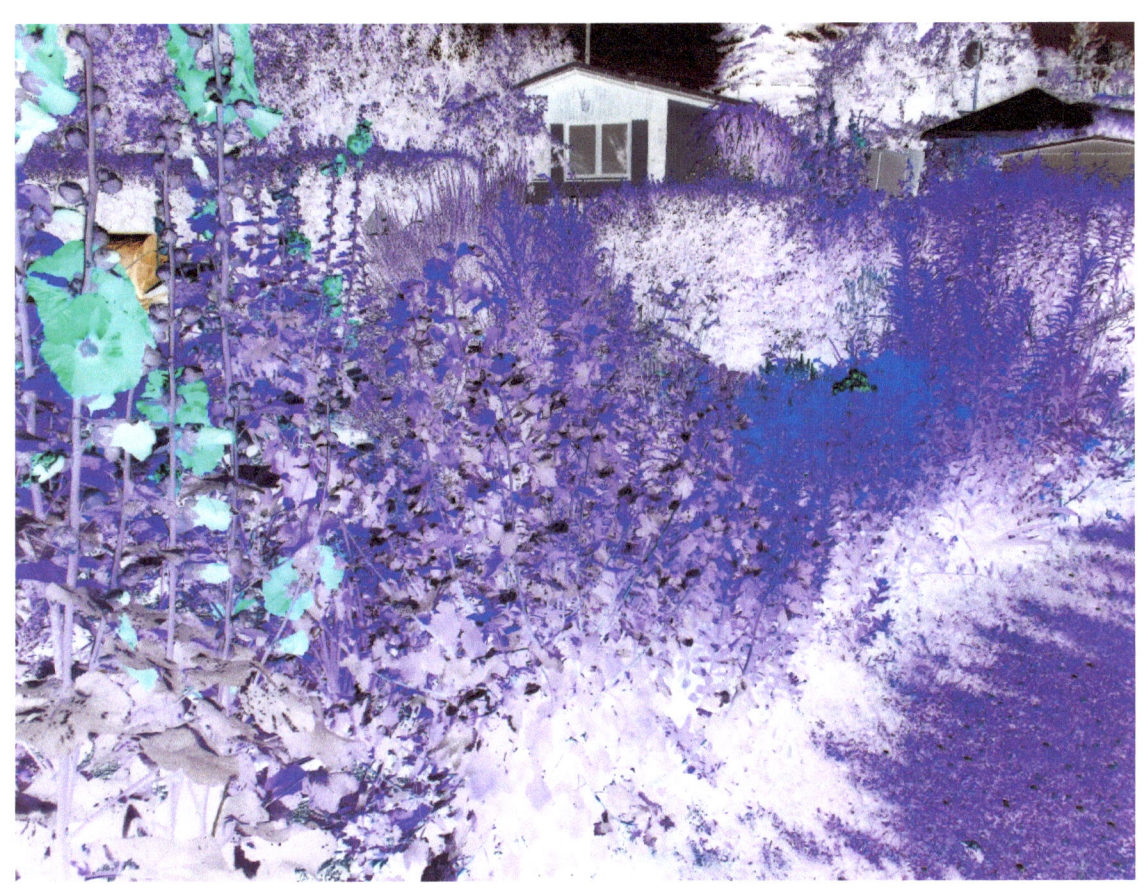
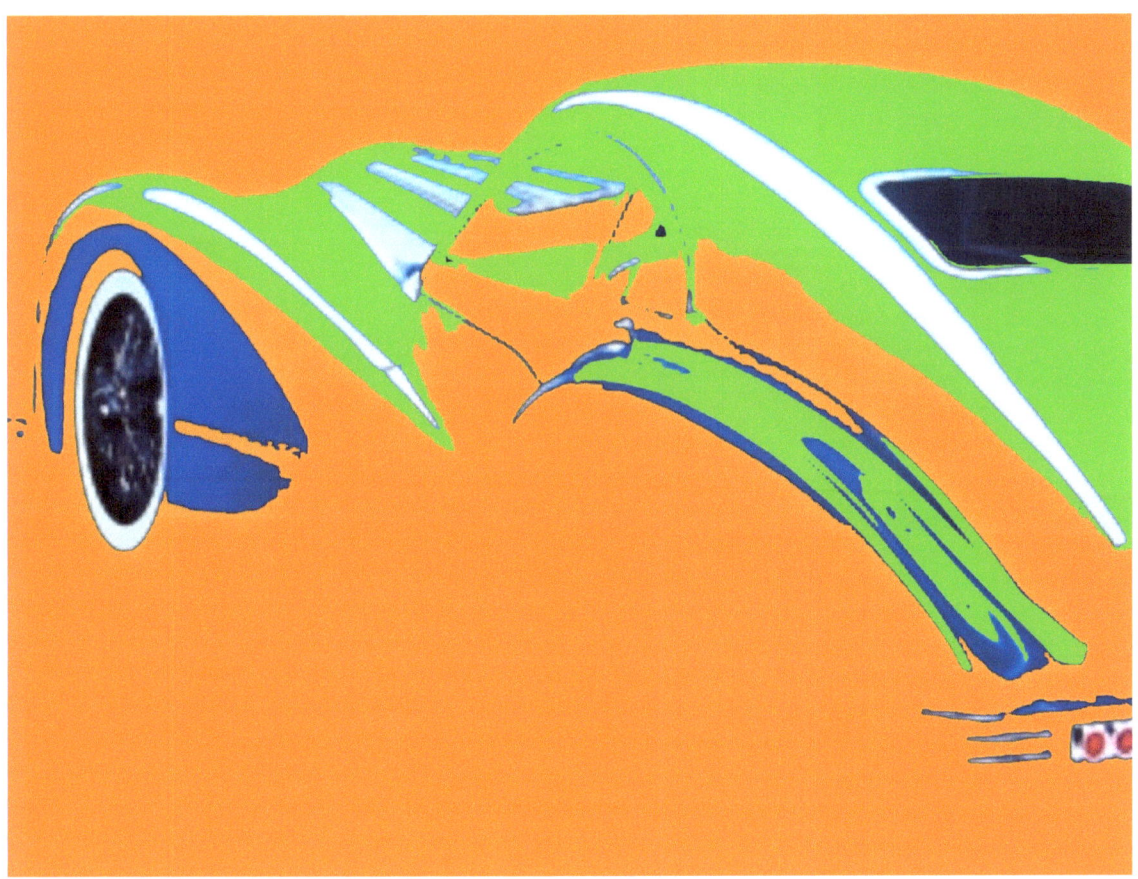

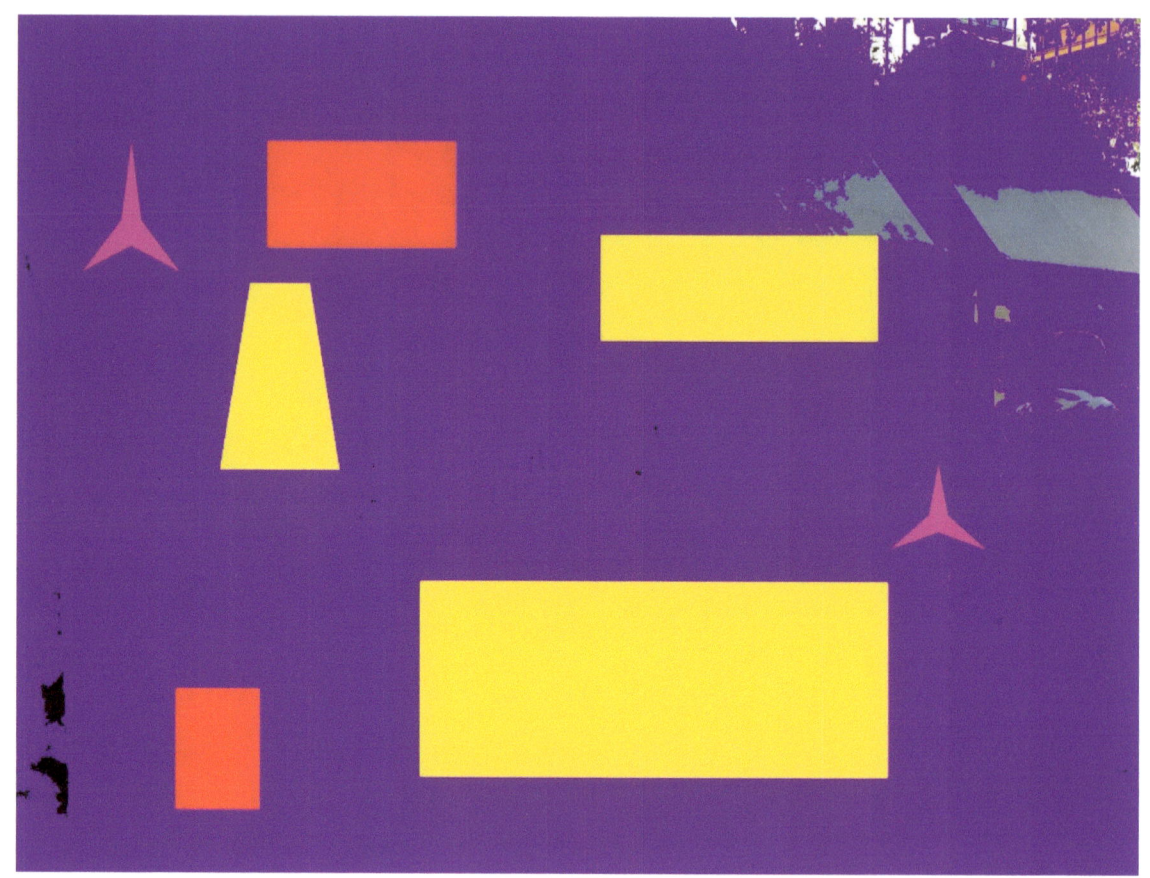
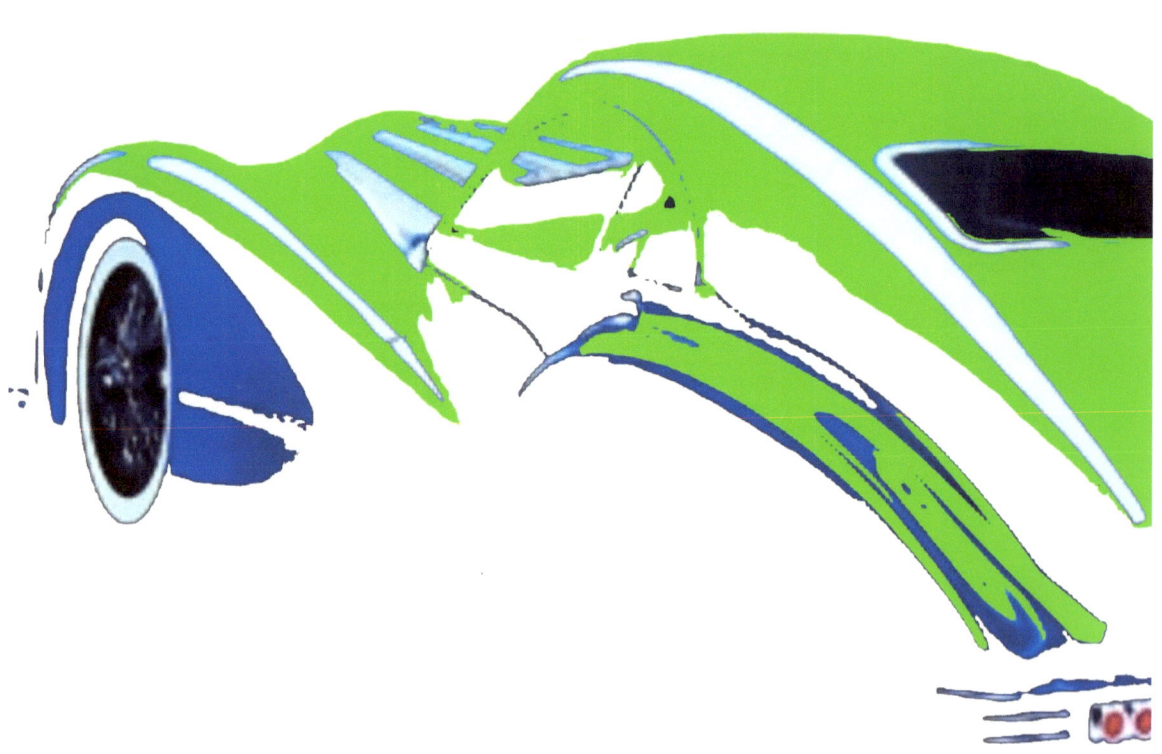

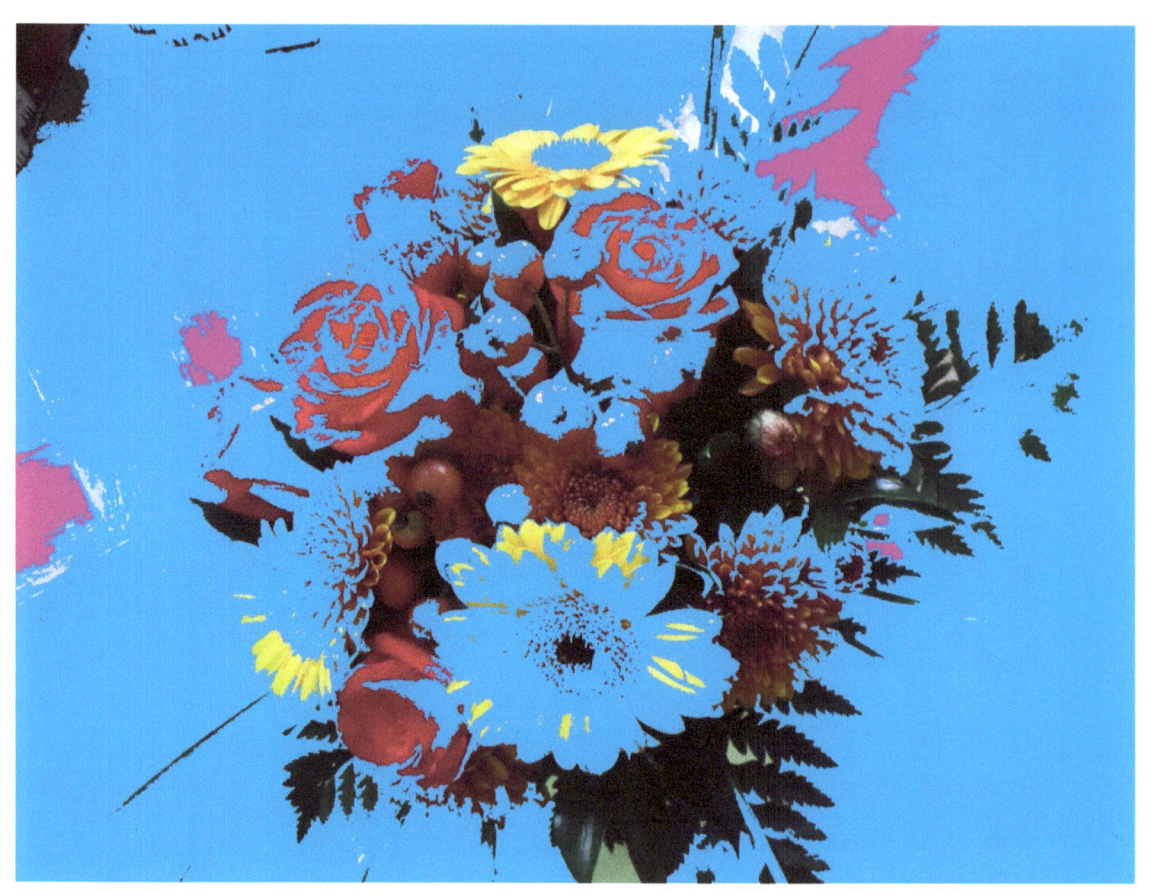
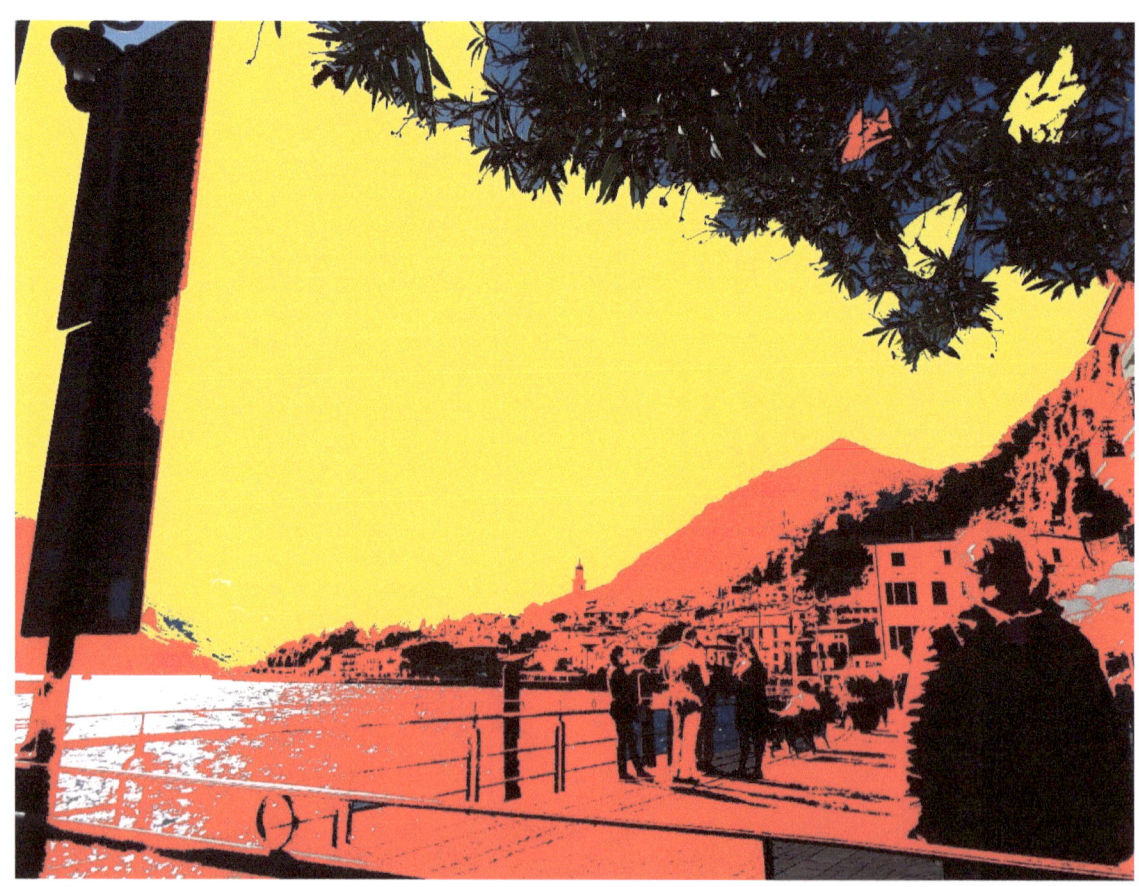

Eckhard Schmittner

SCHLEMITZ

75 Kurzgeschichten

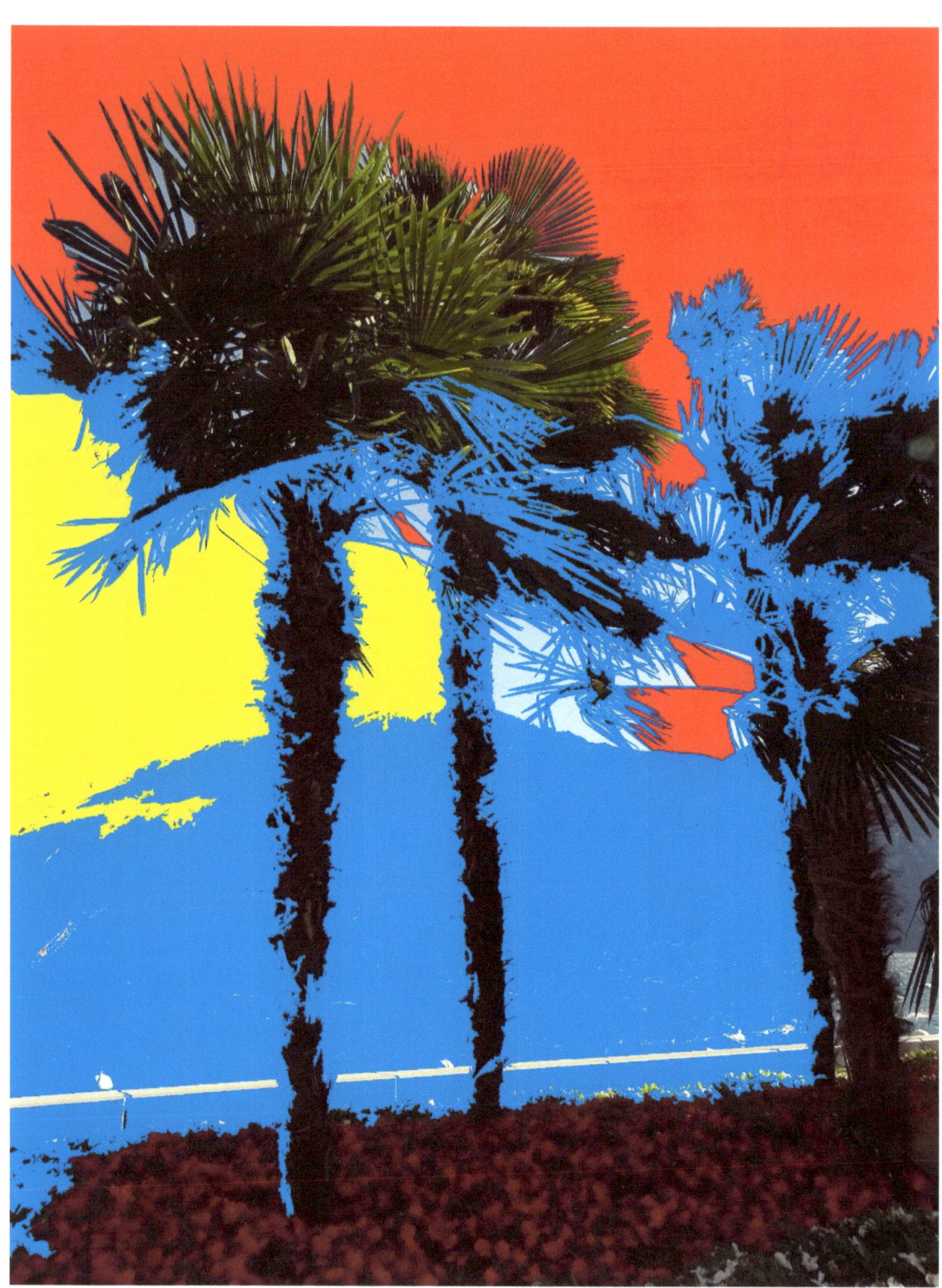

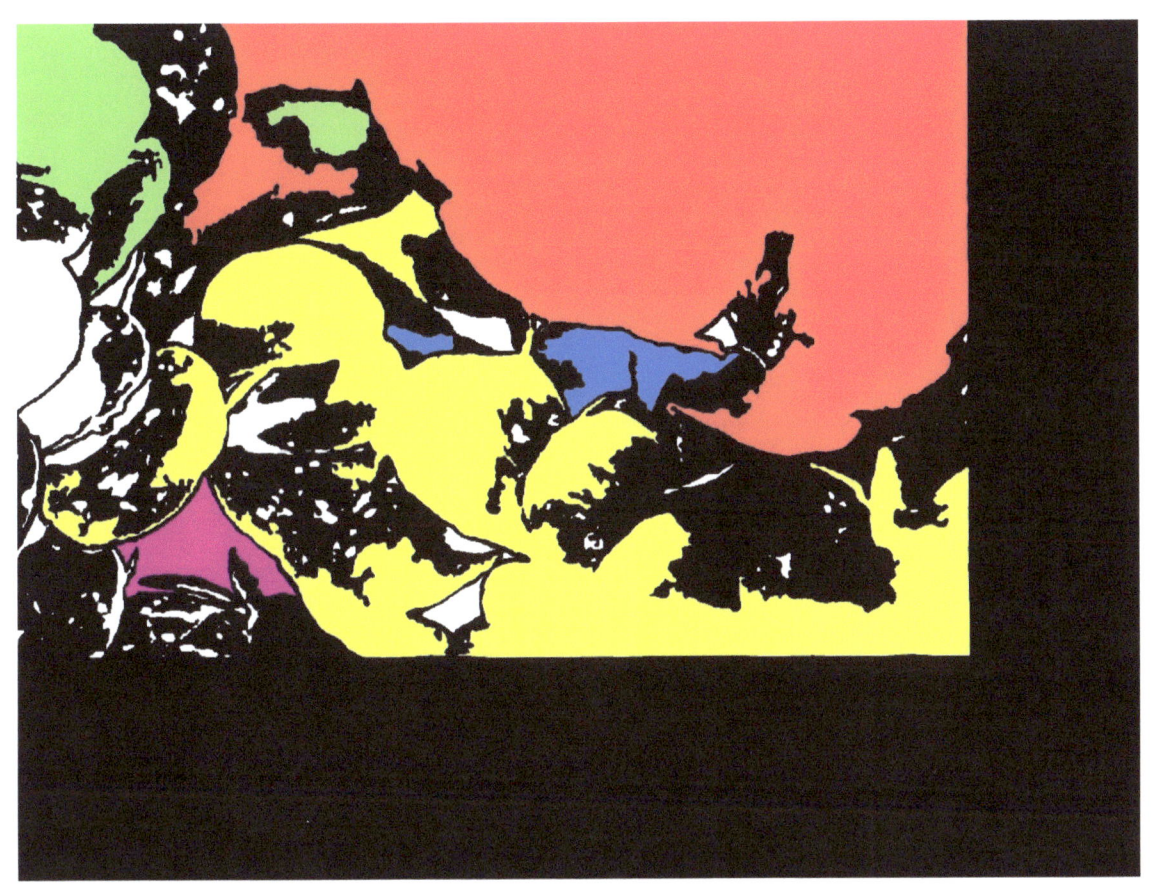
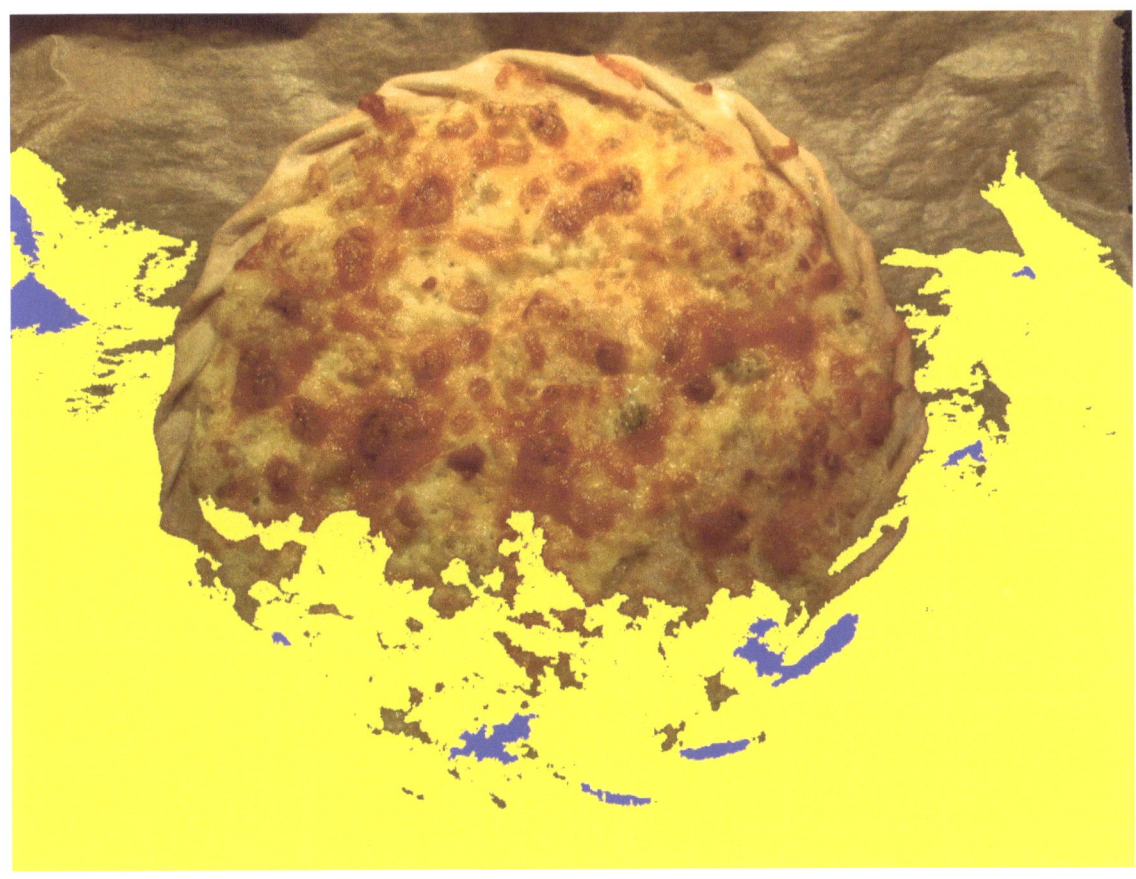

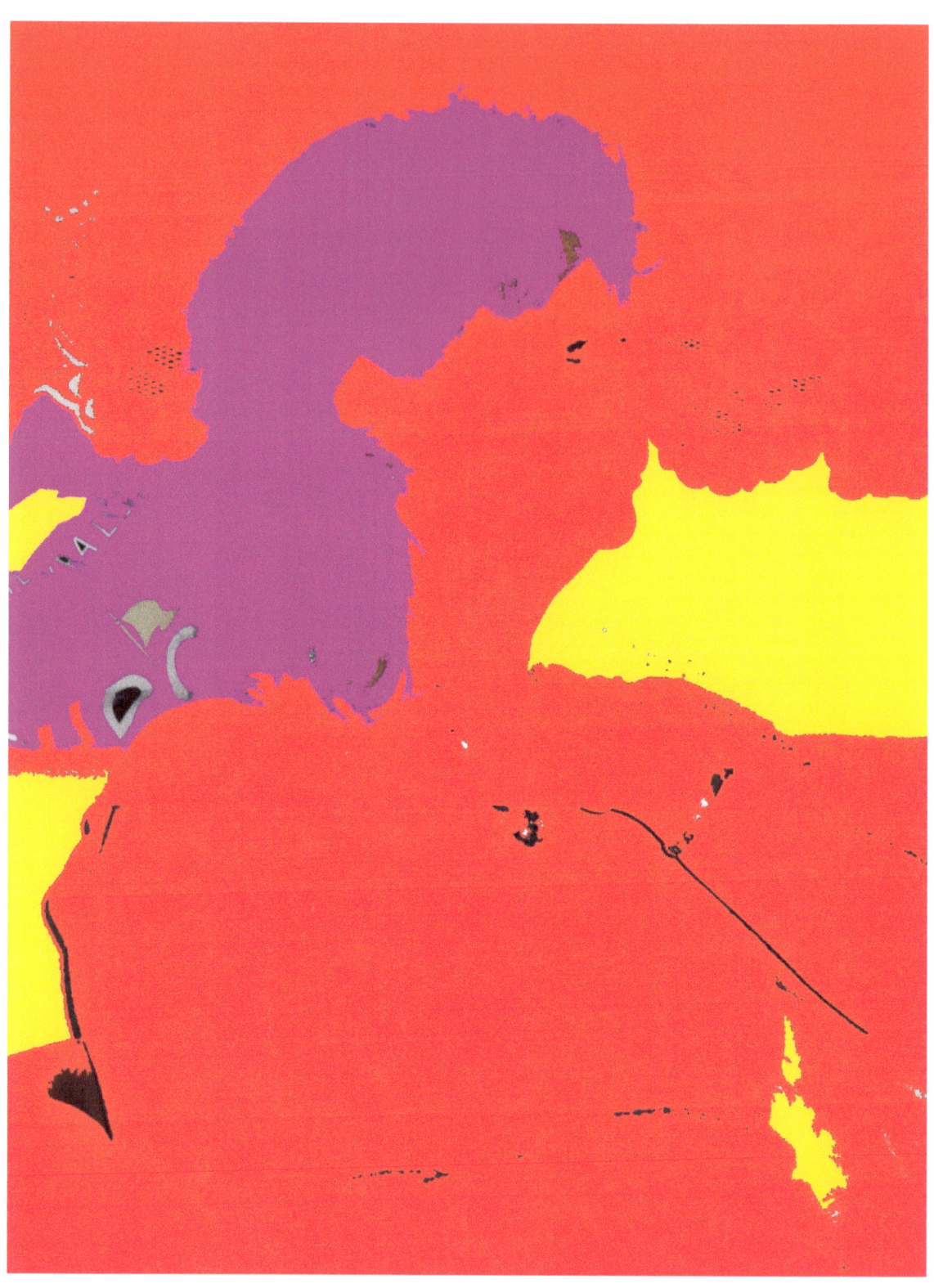

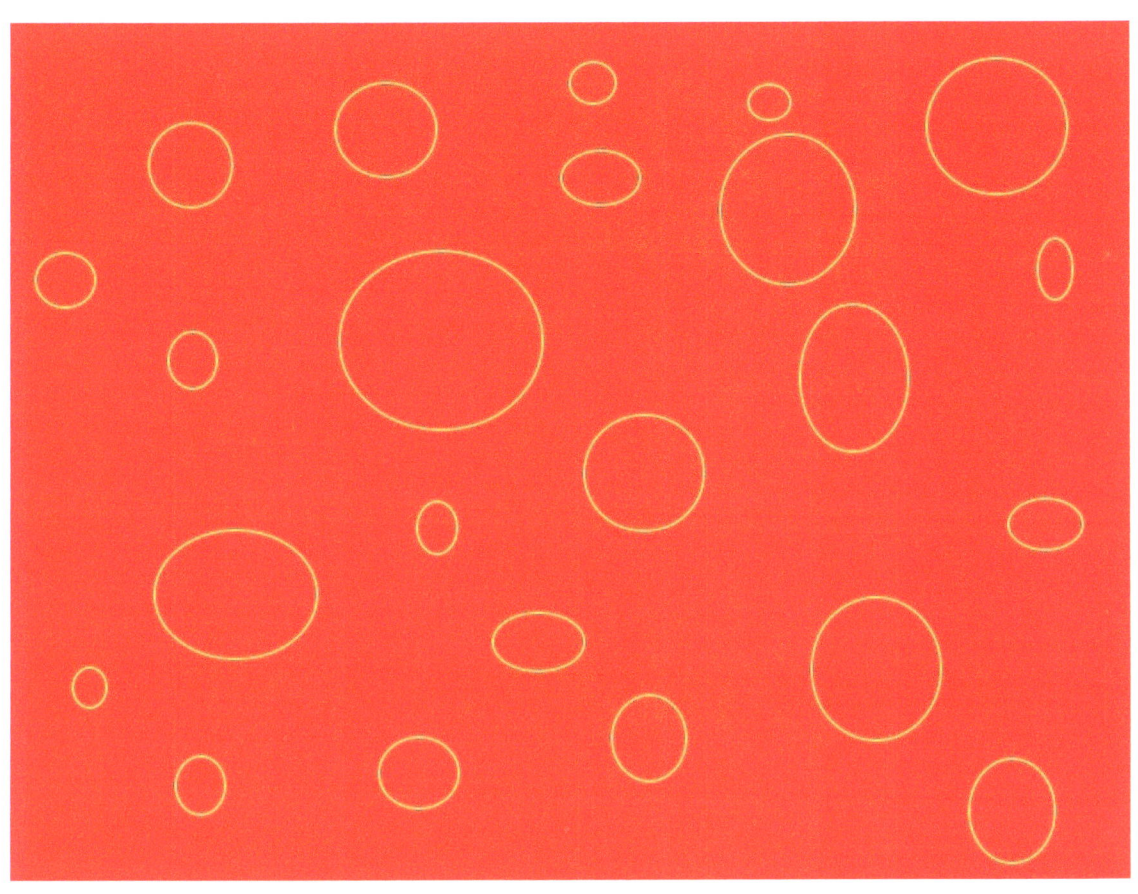

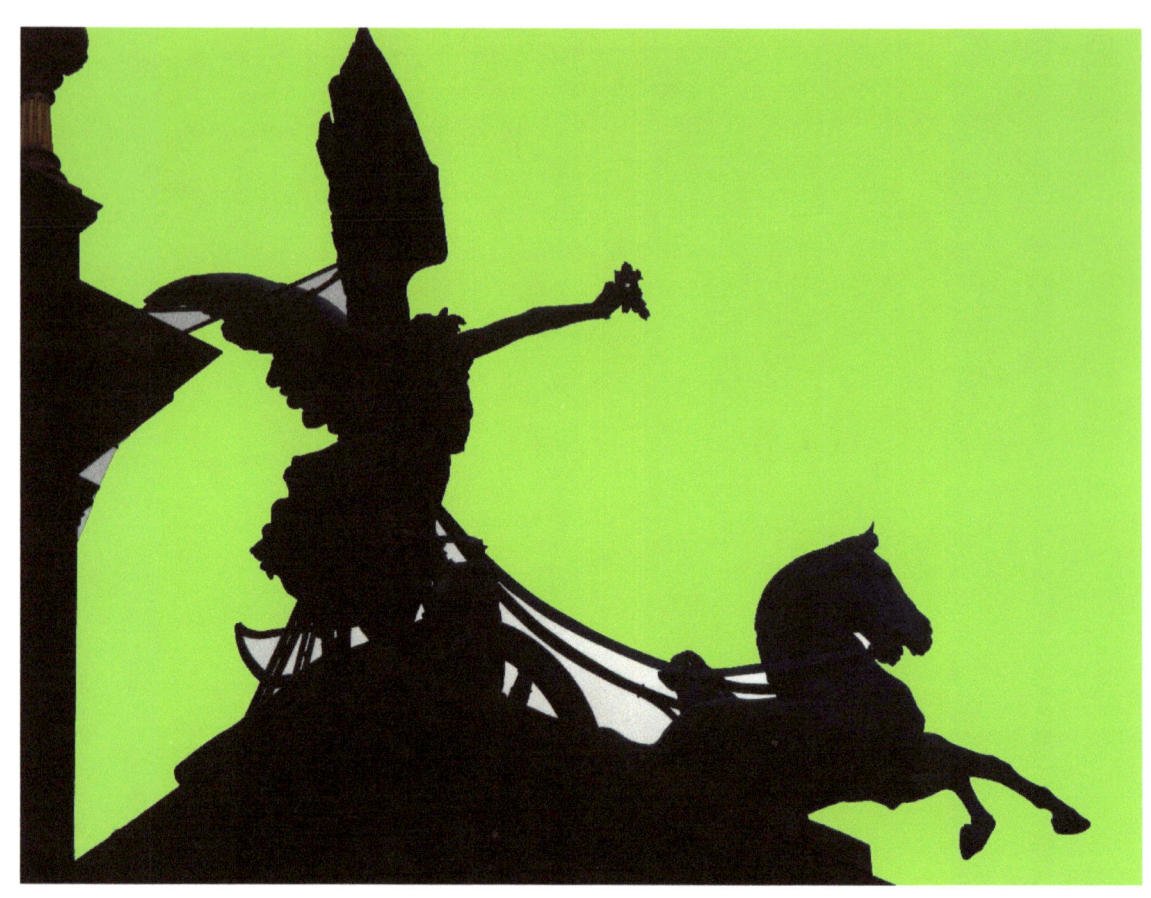

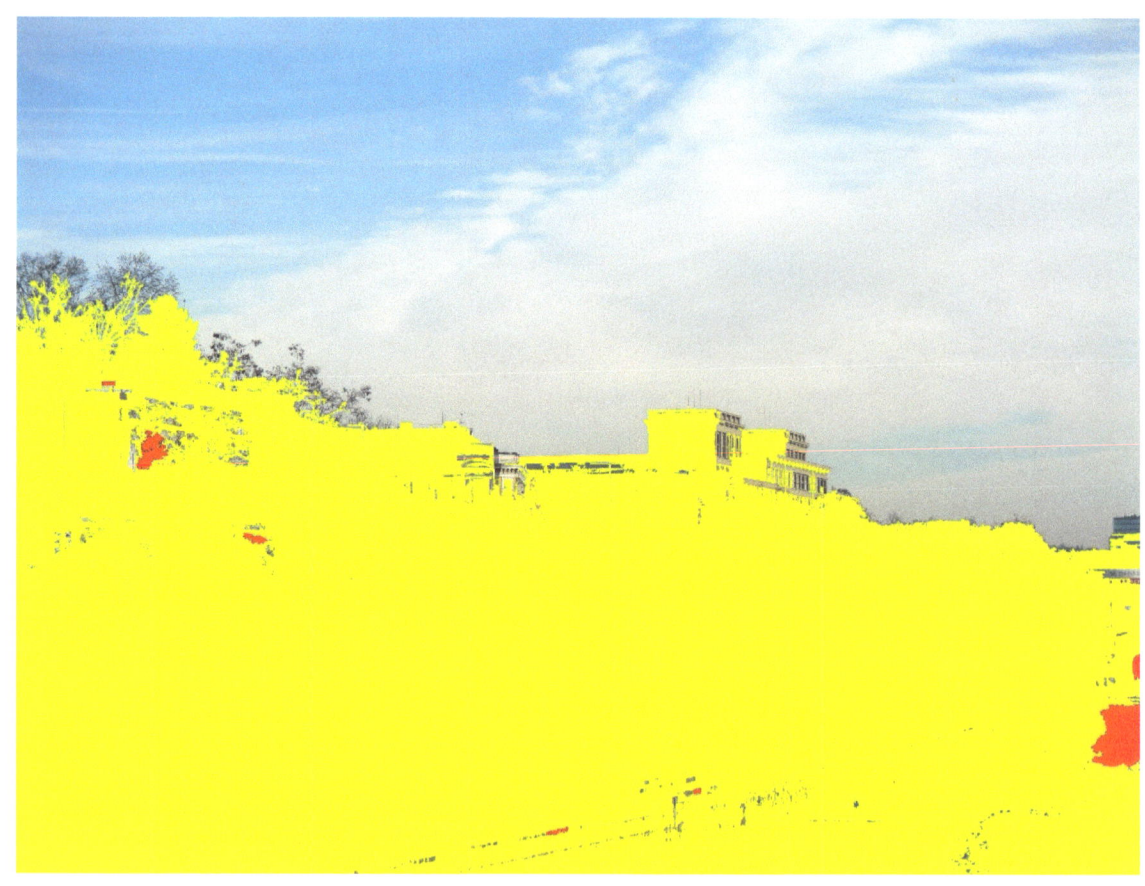

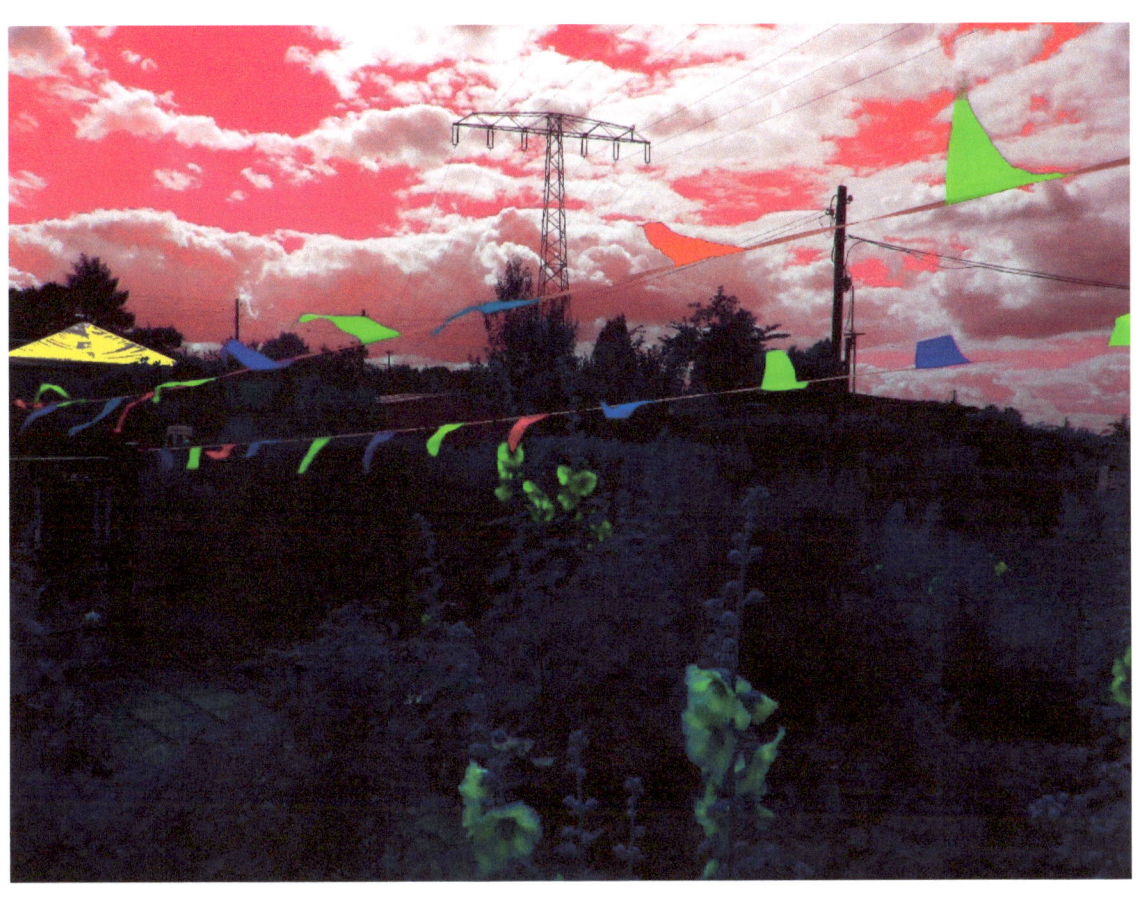

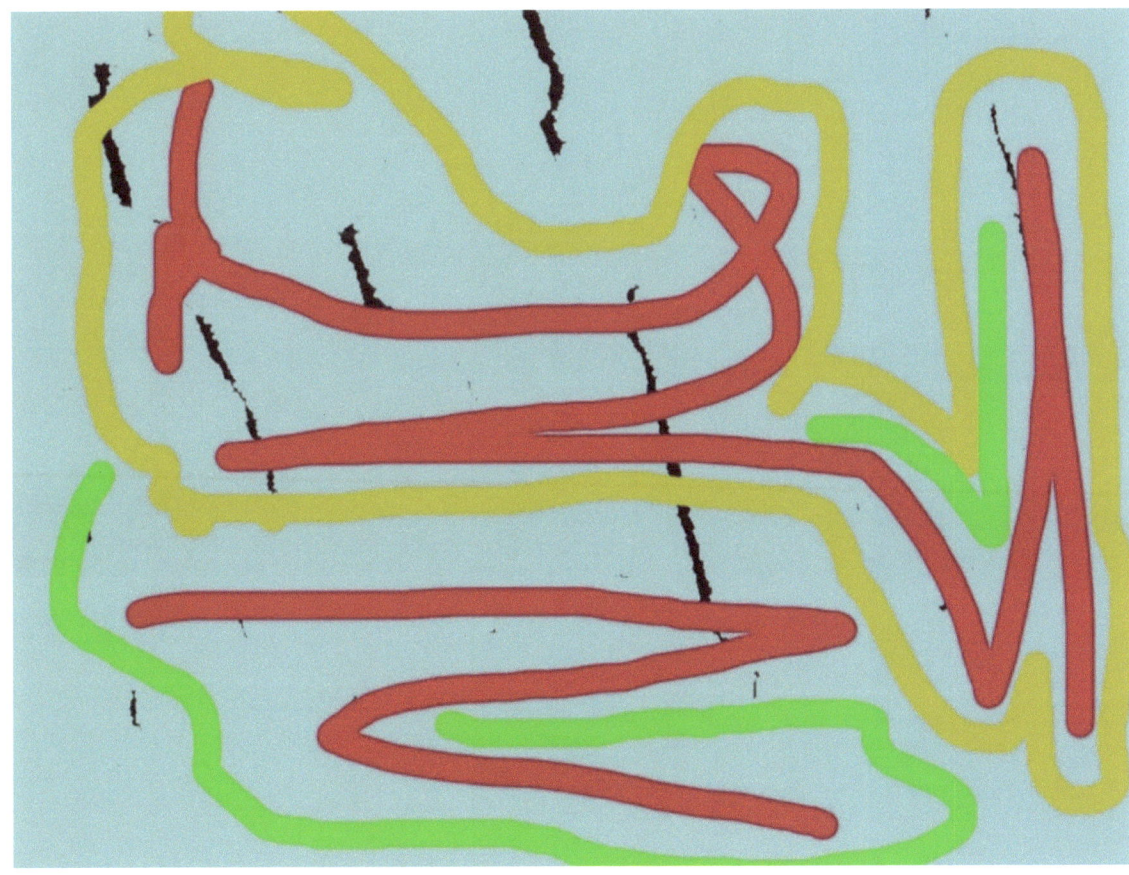

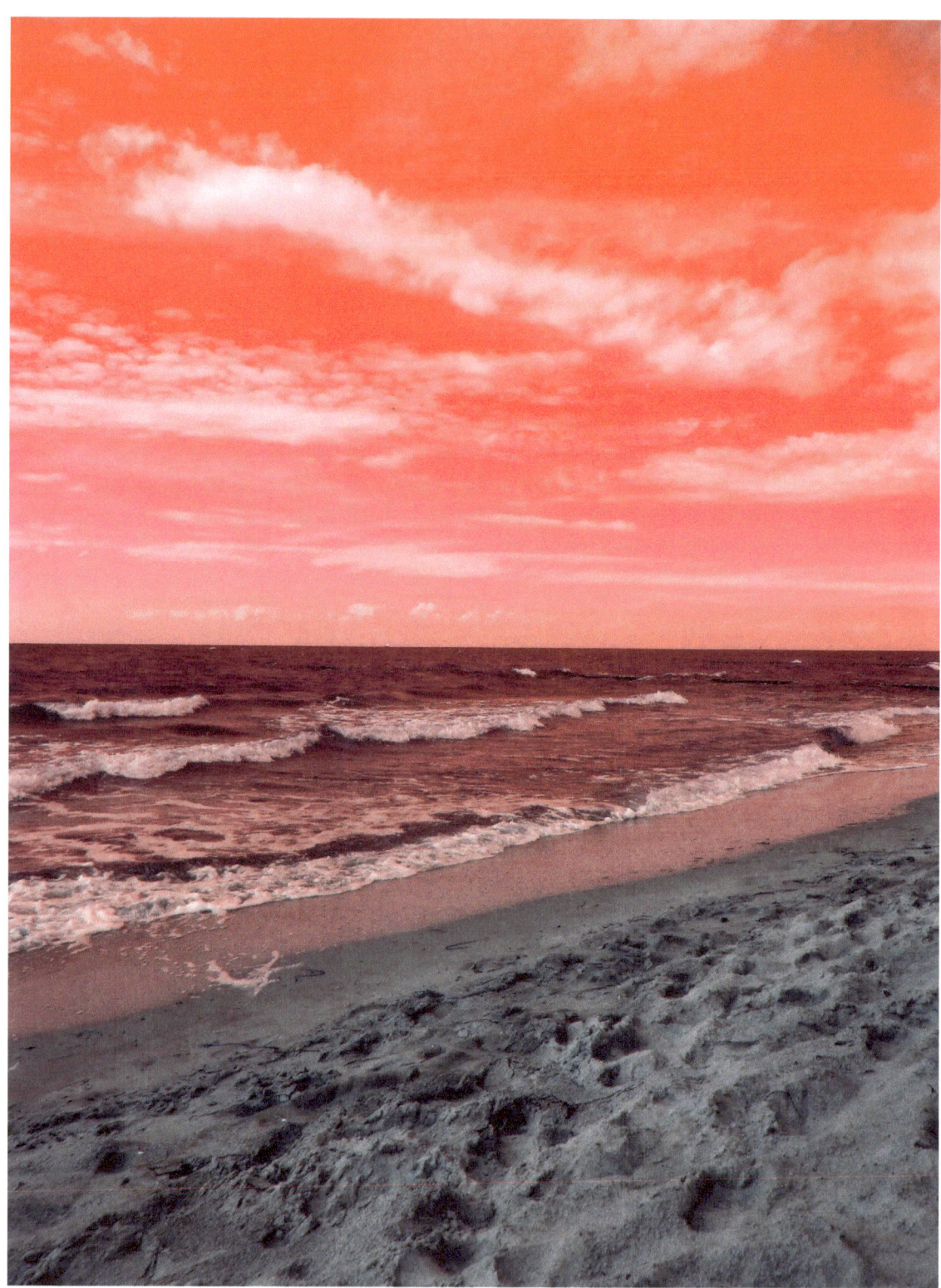

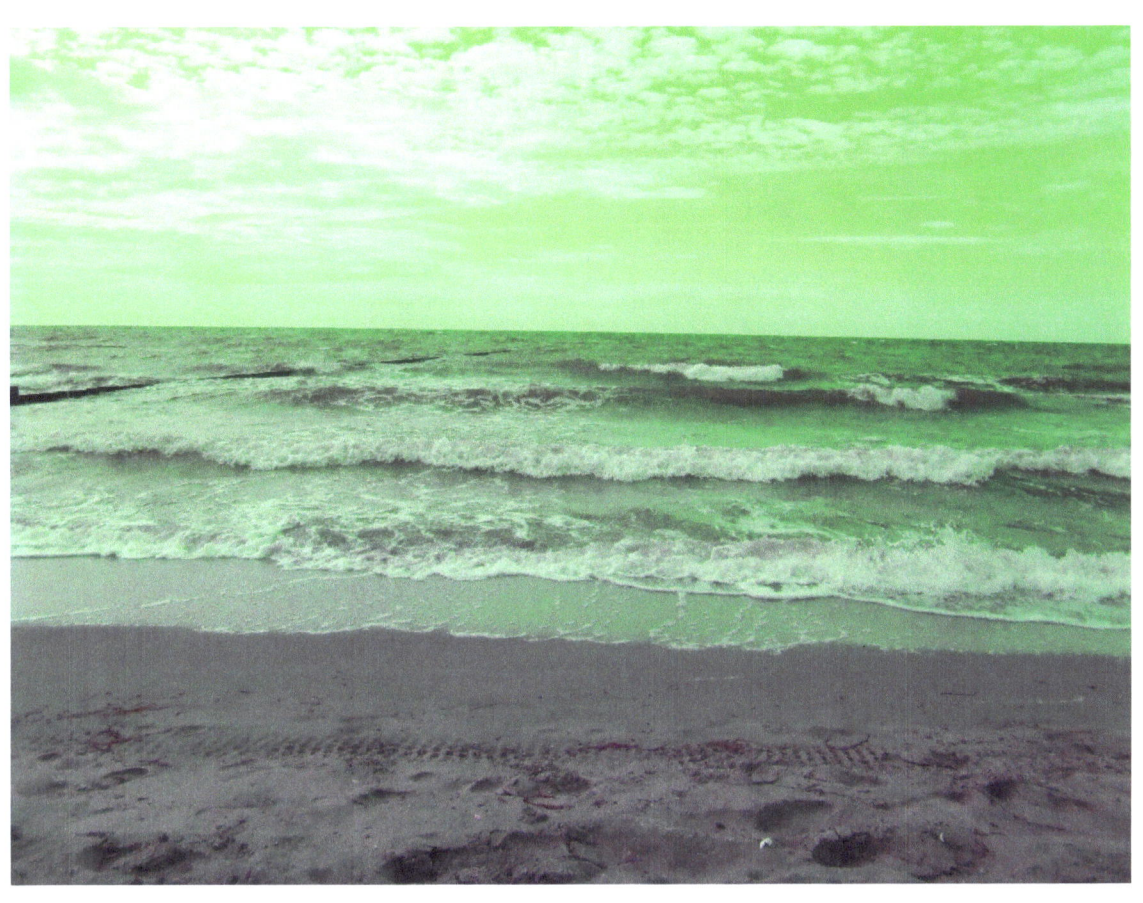

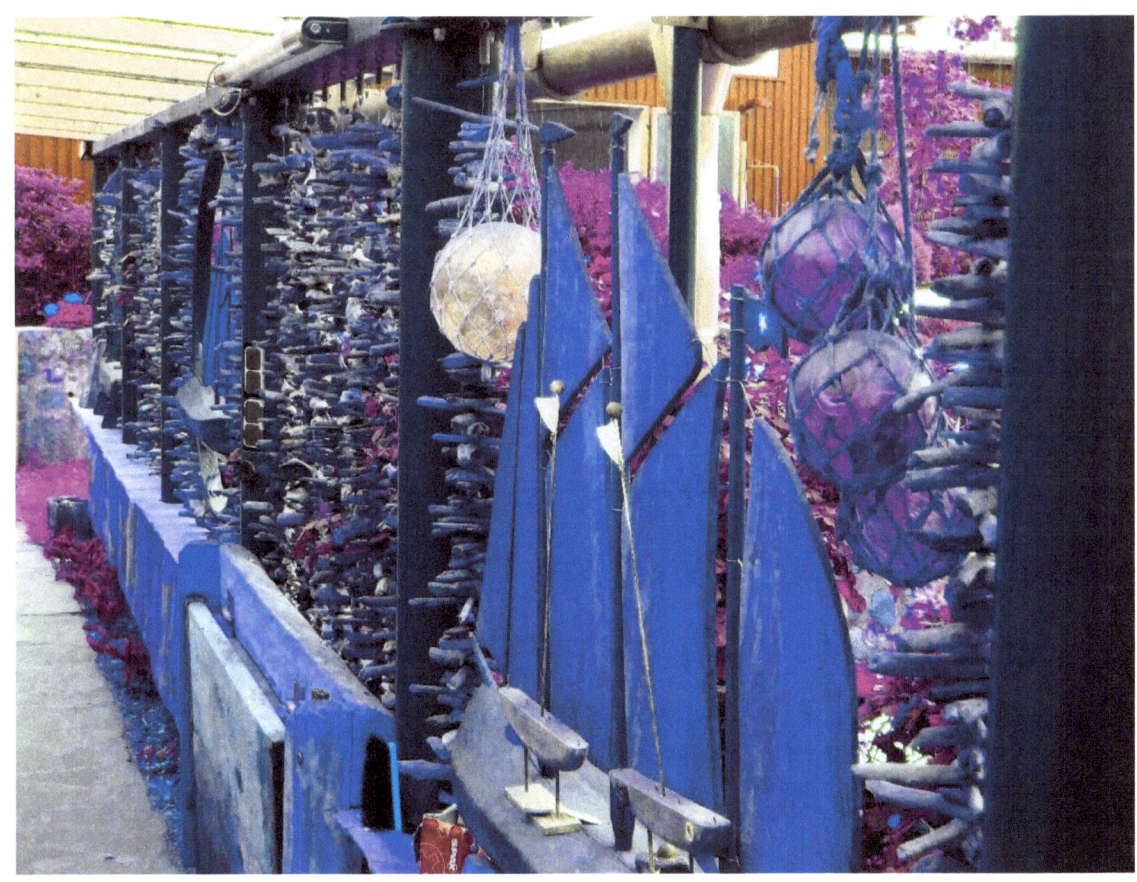

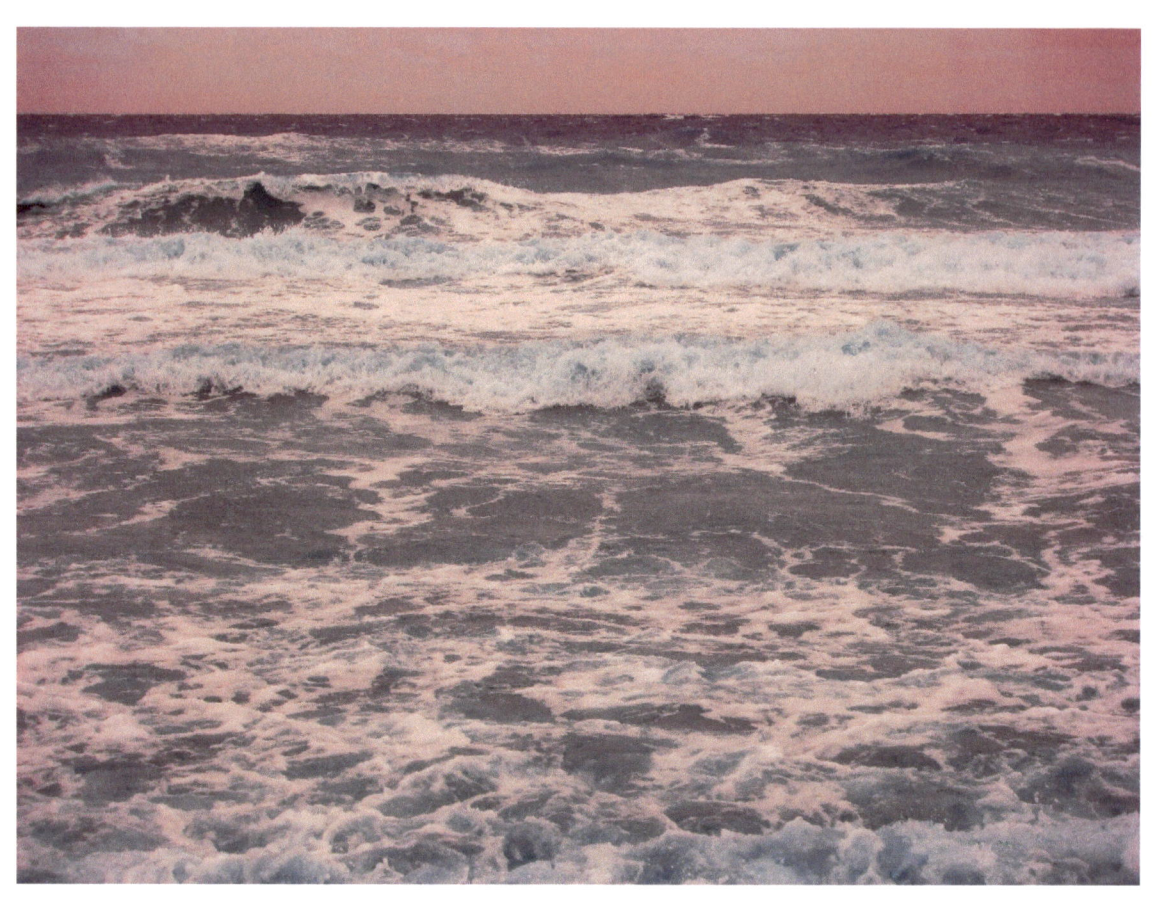
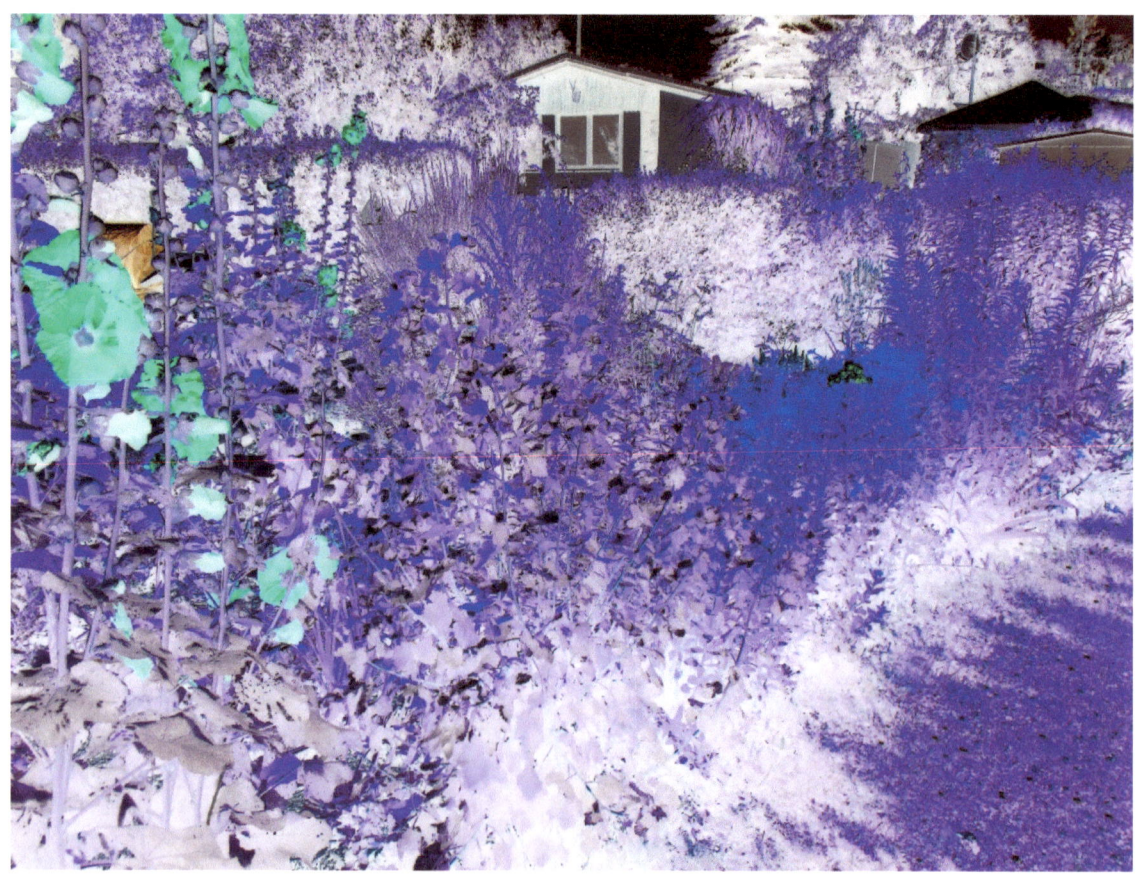

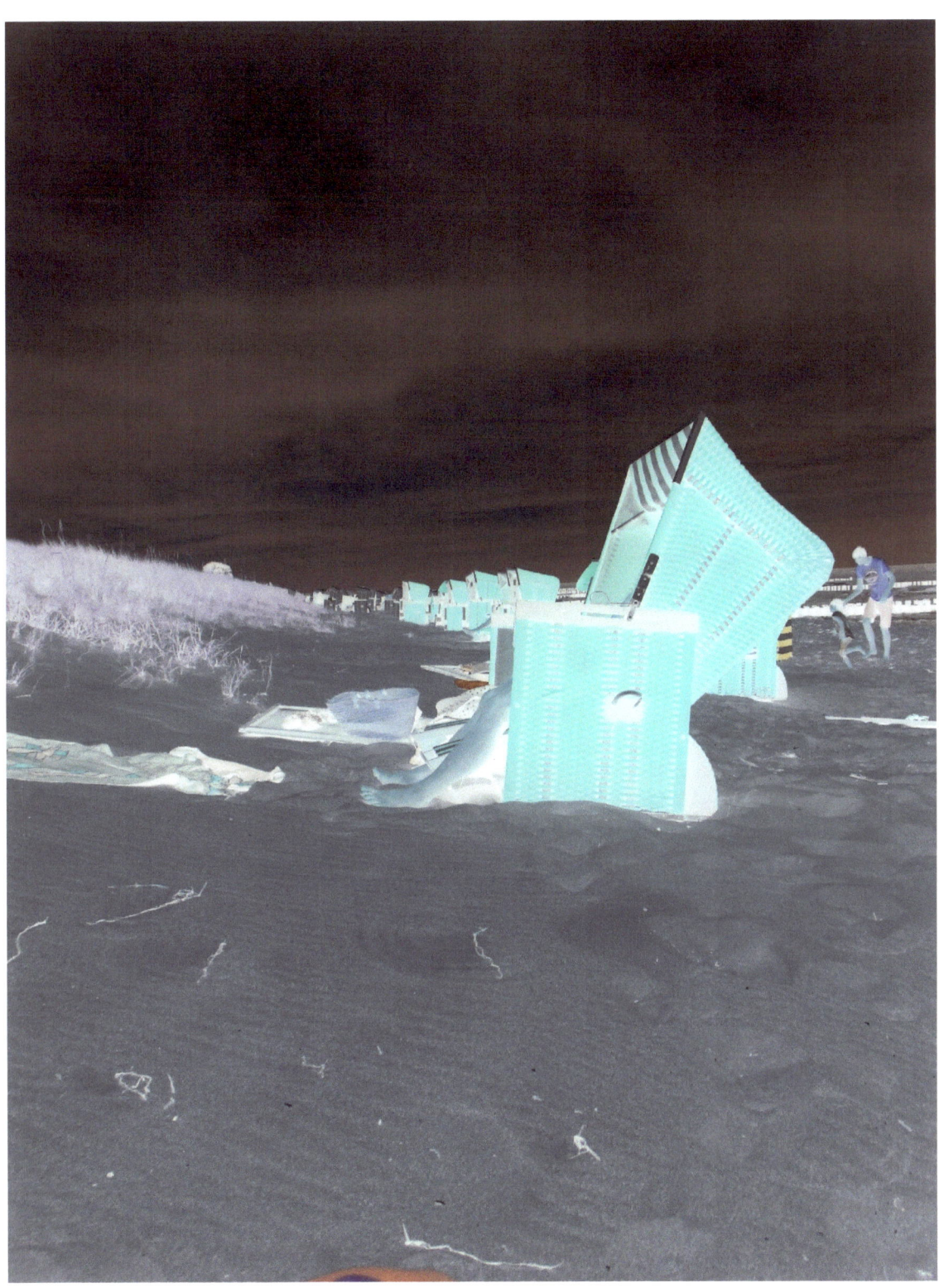

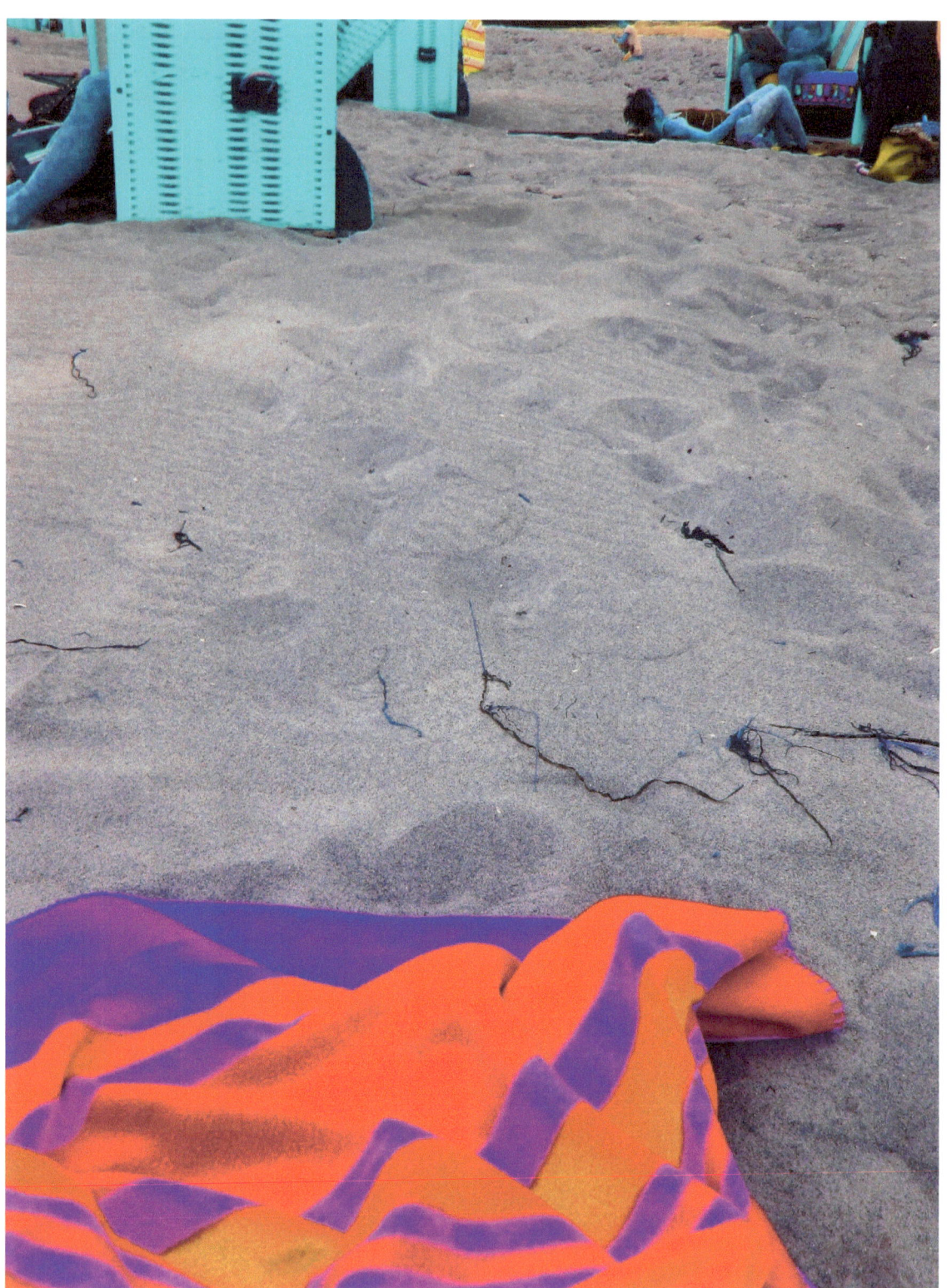

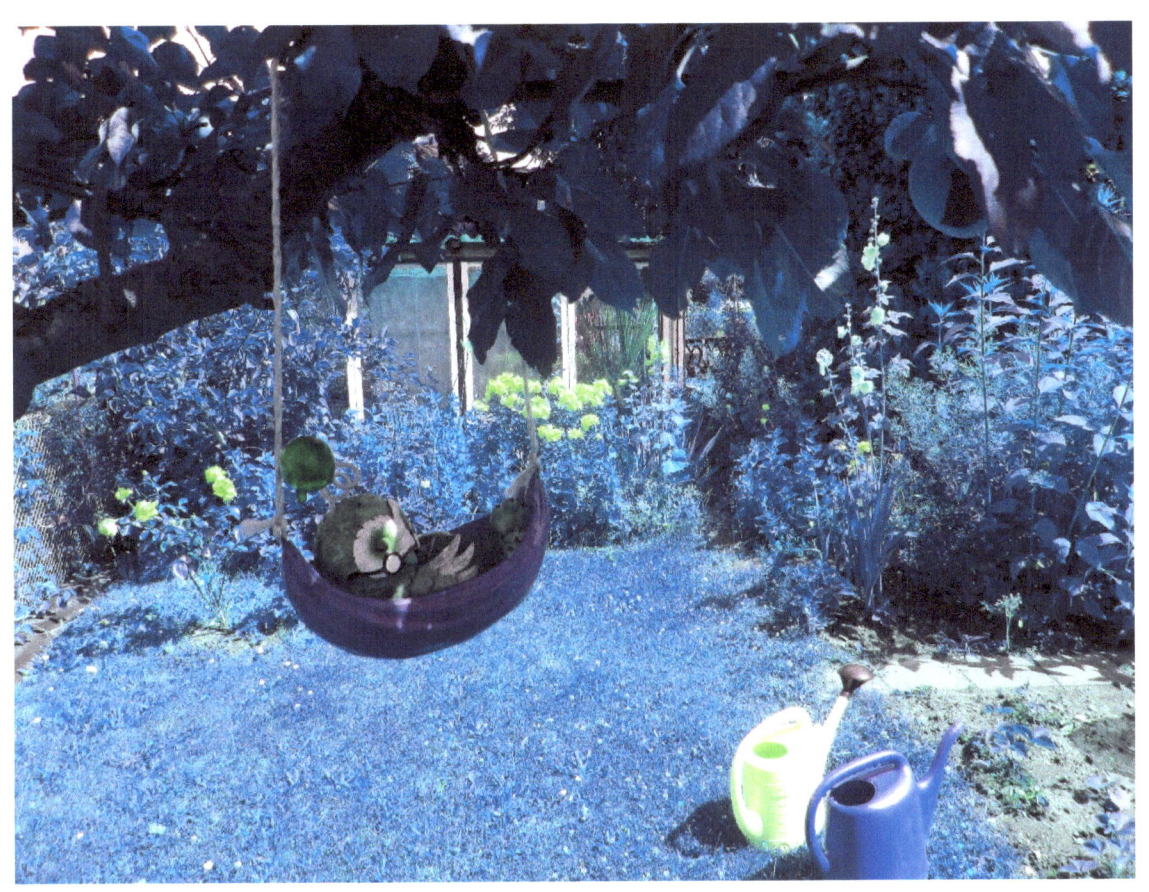
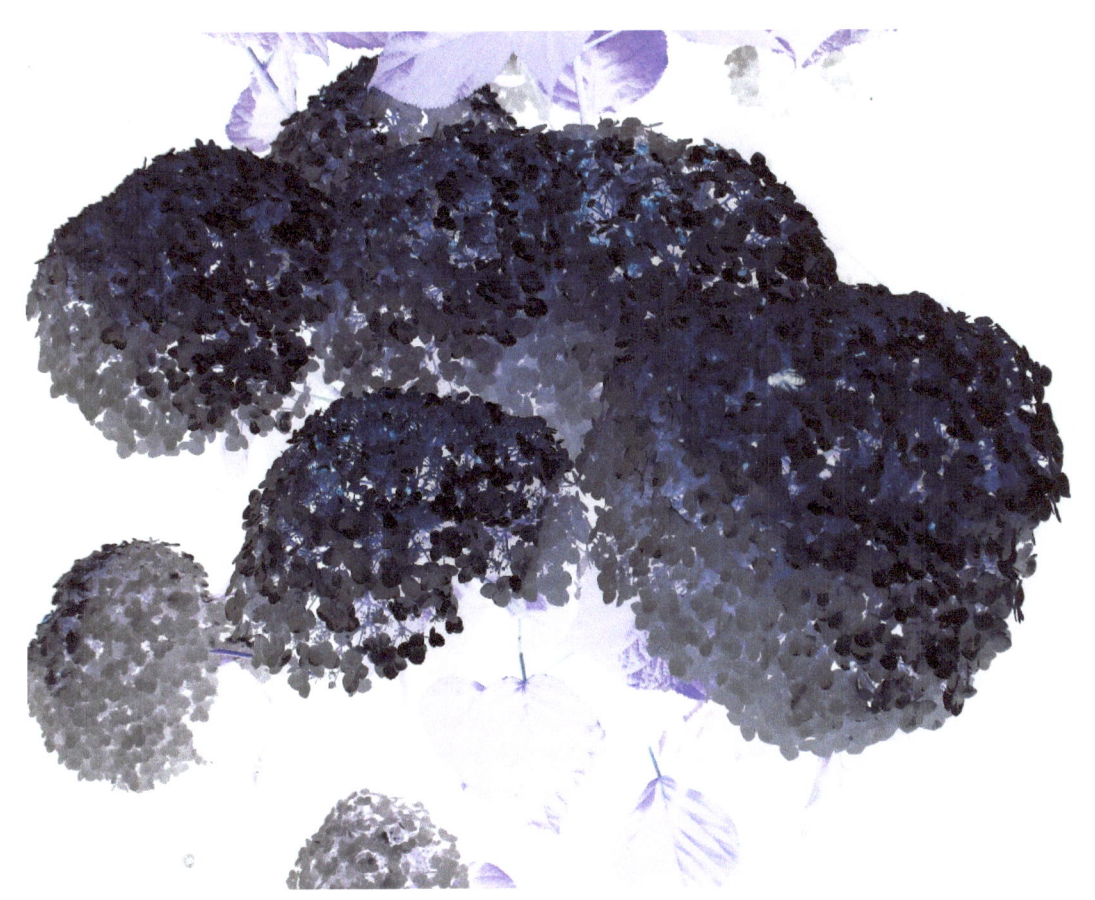

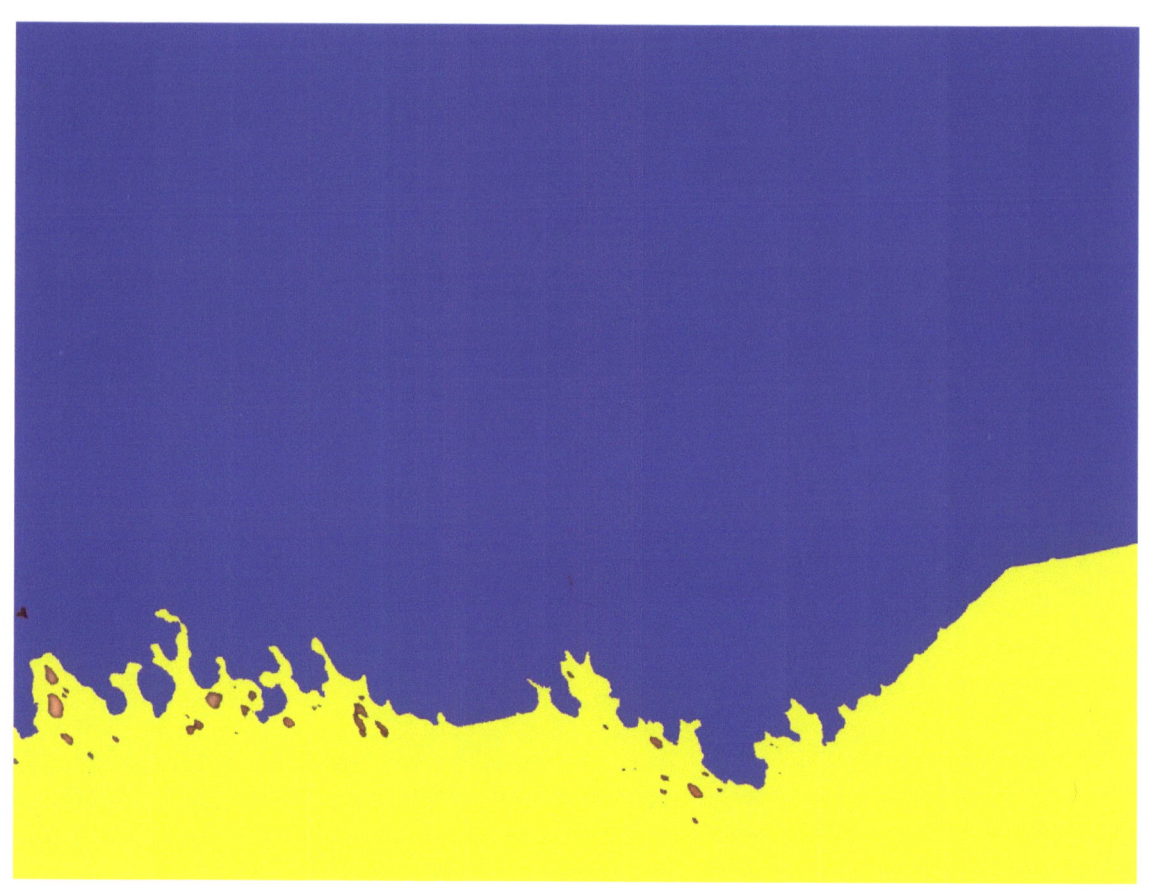
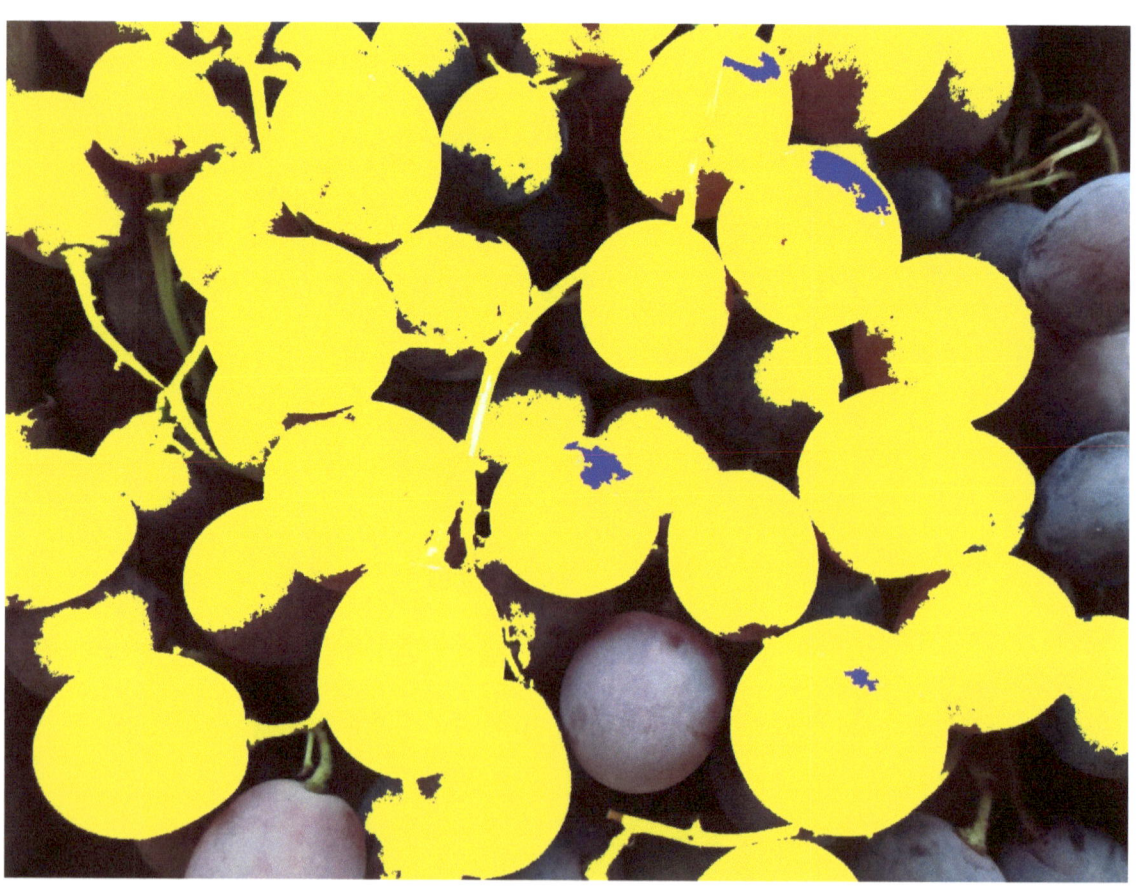

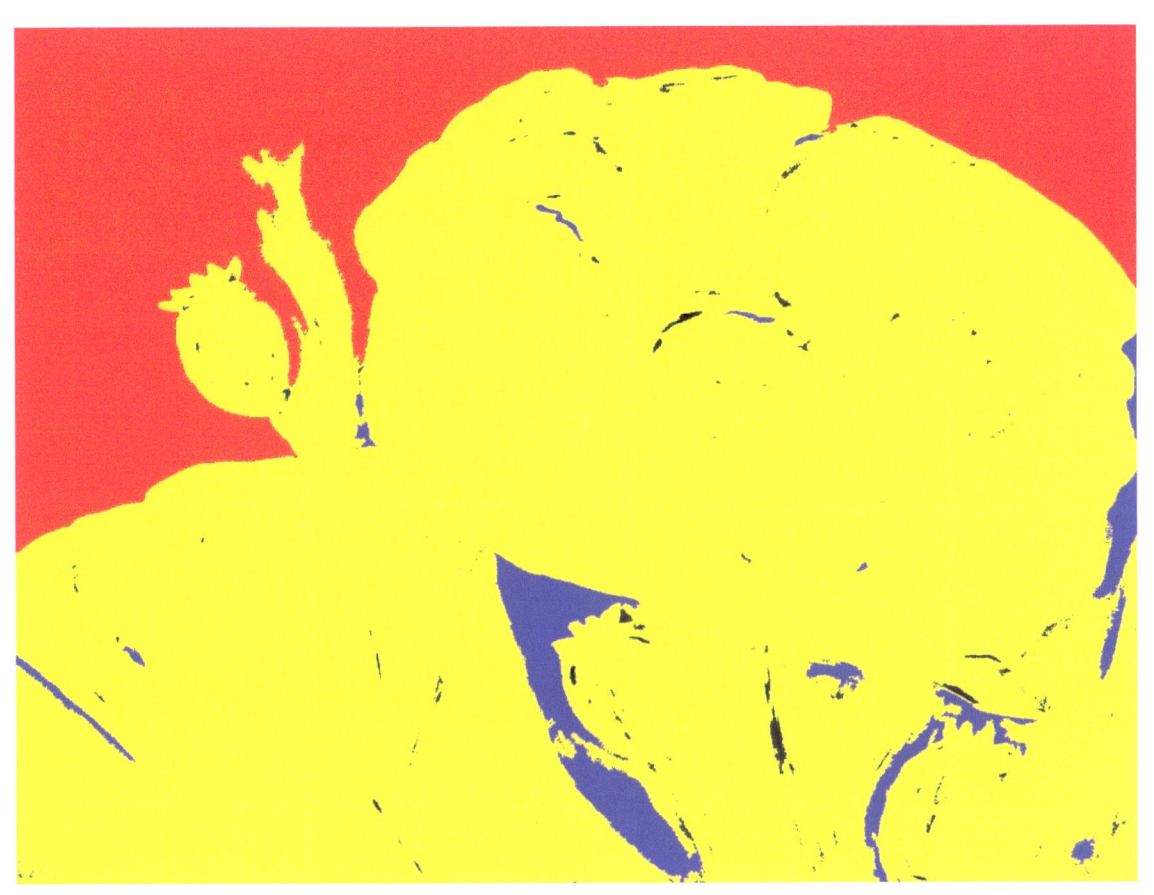
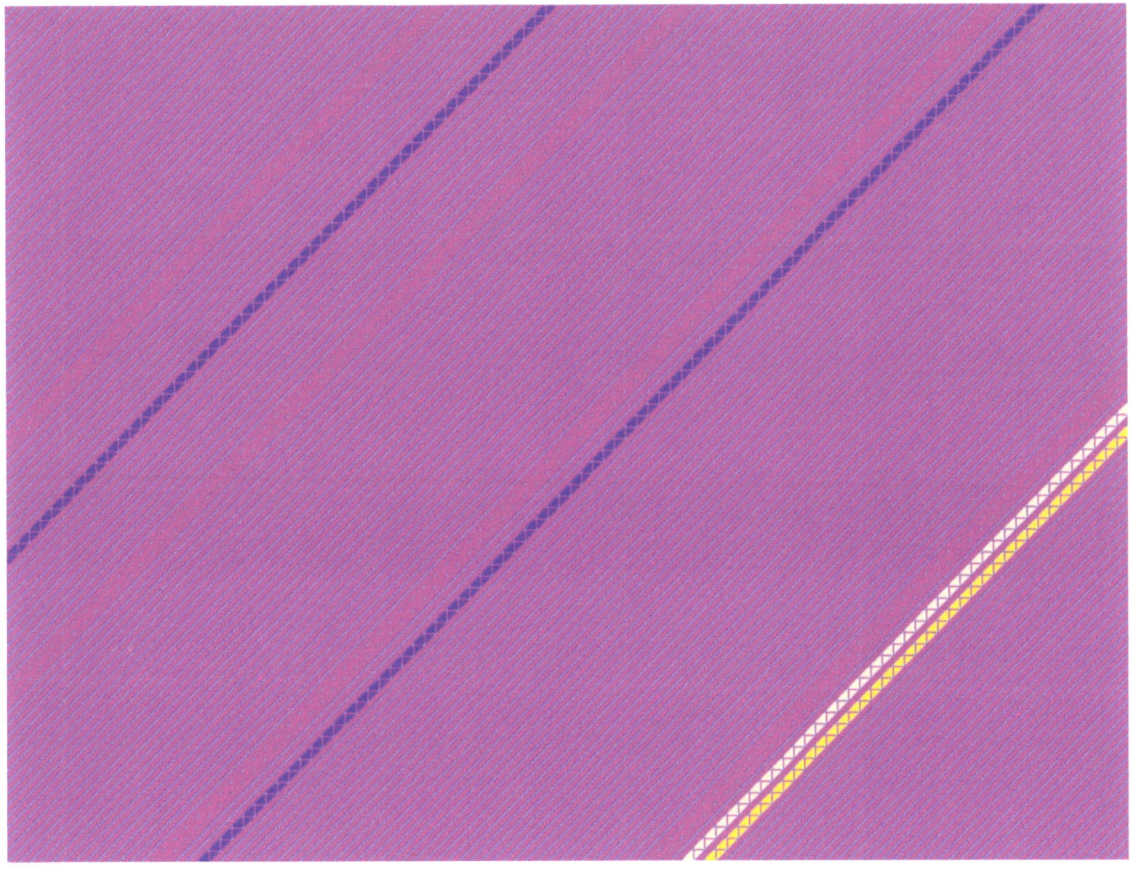

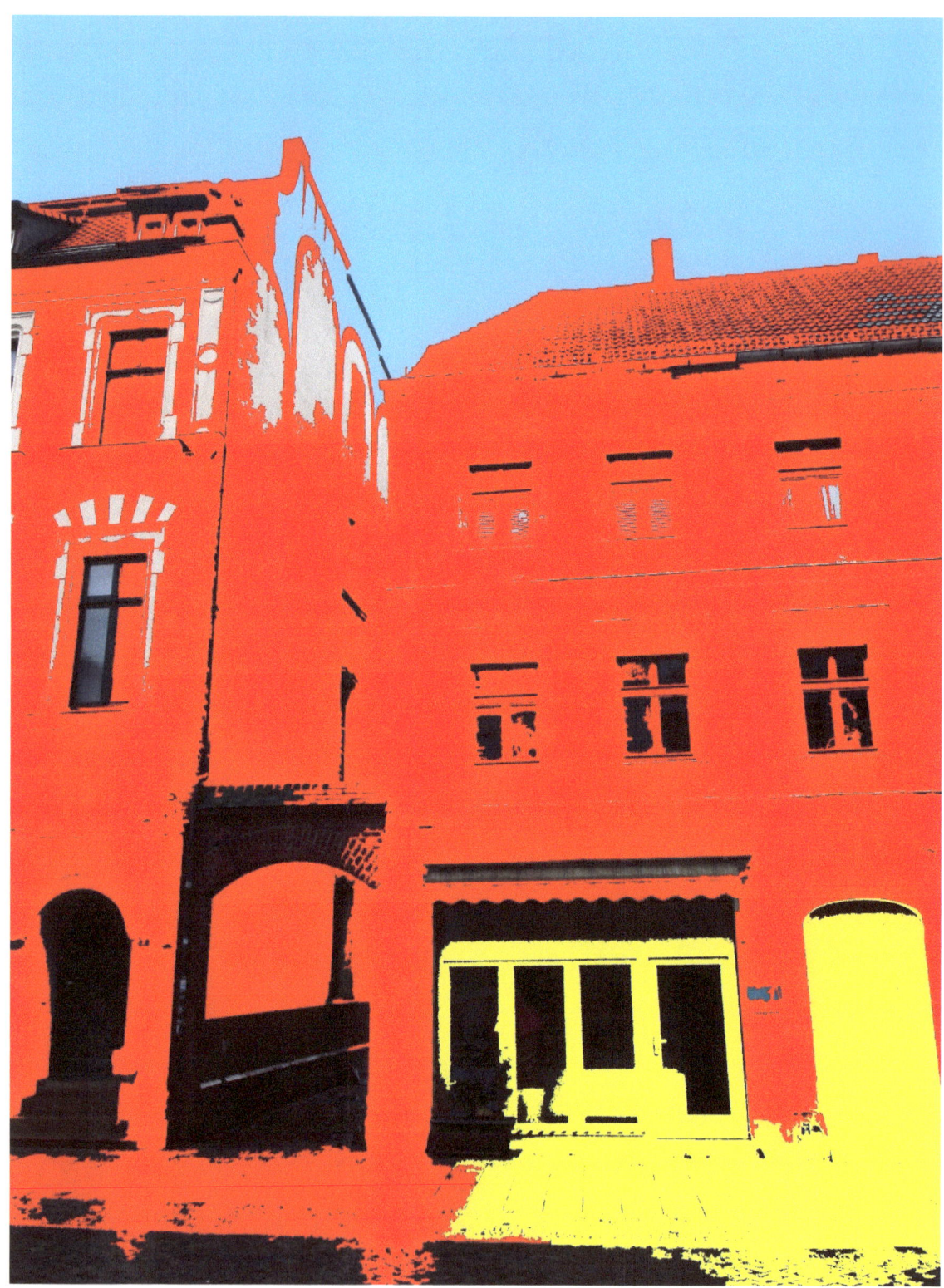

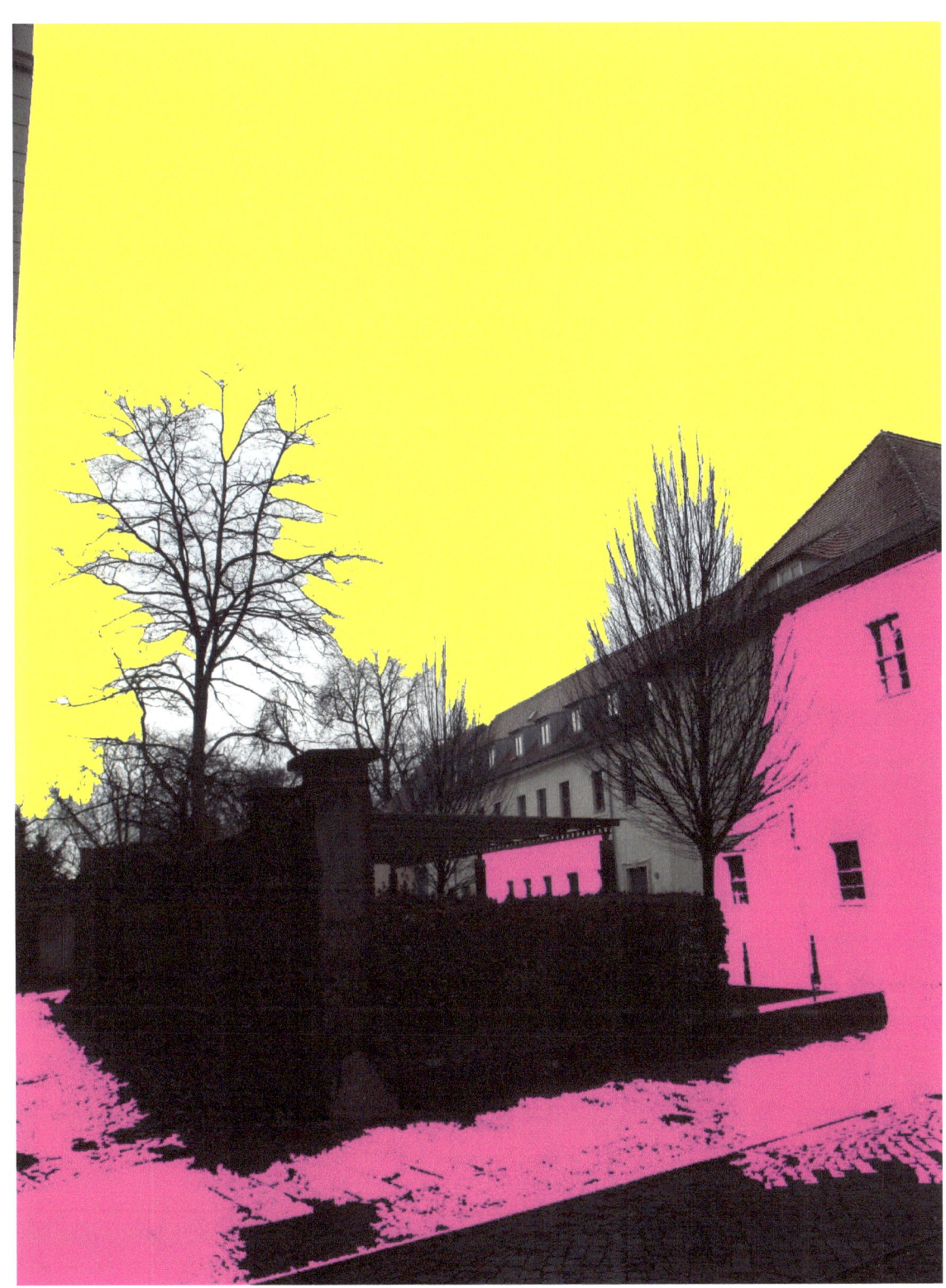

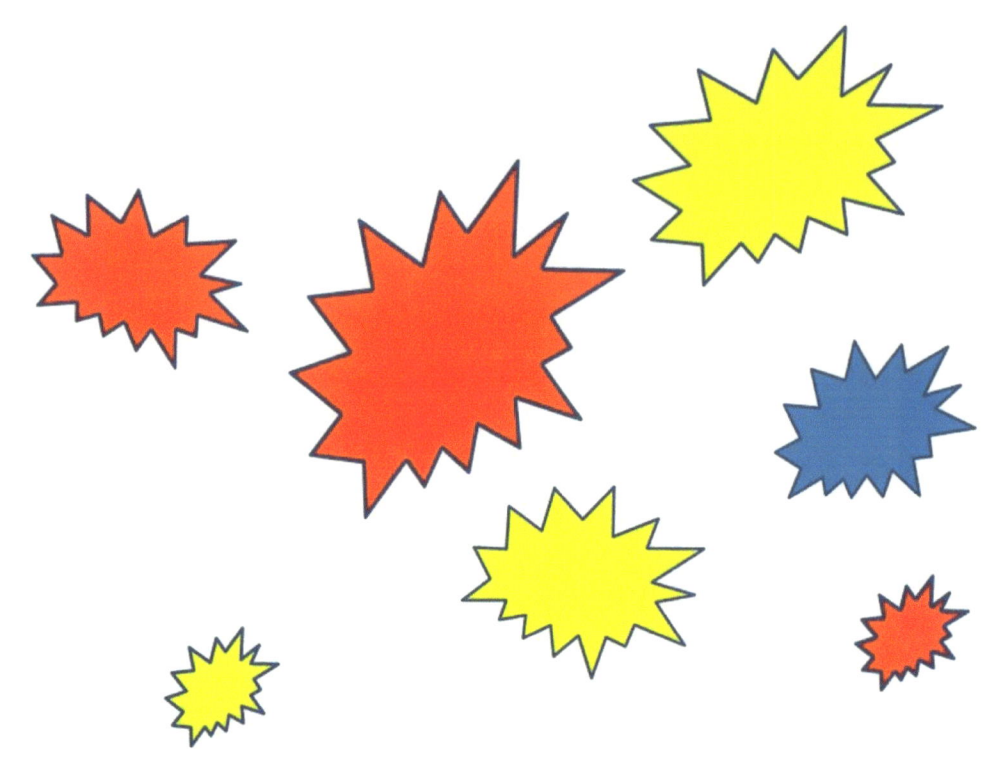
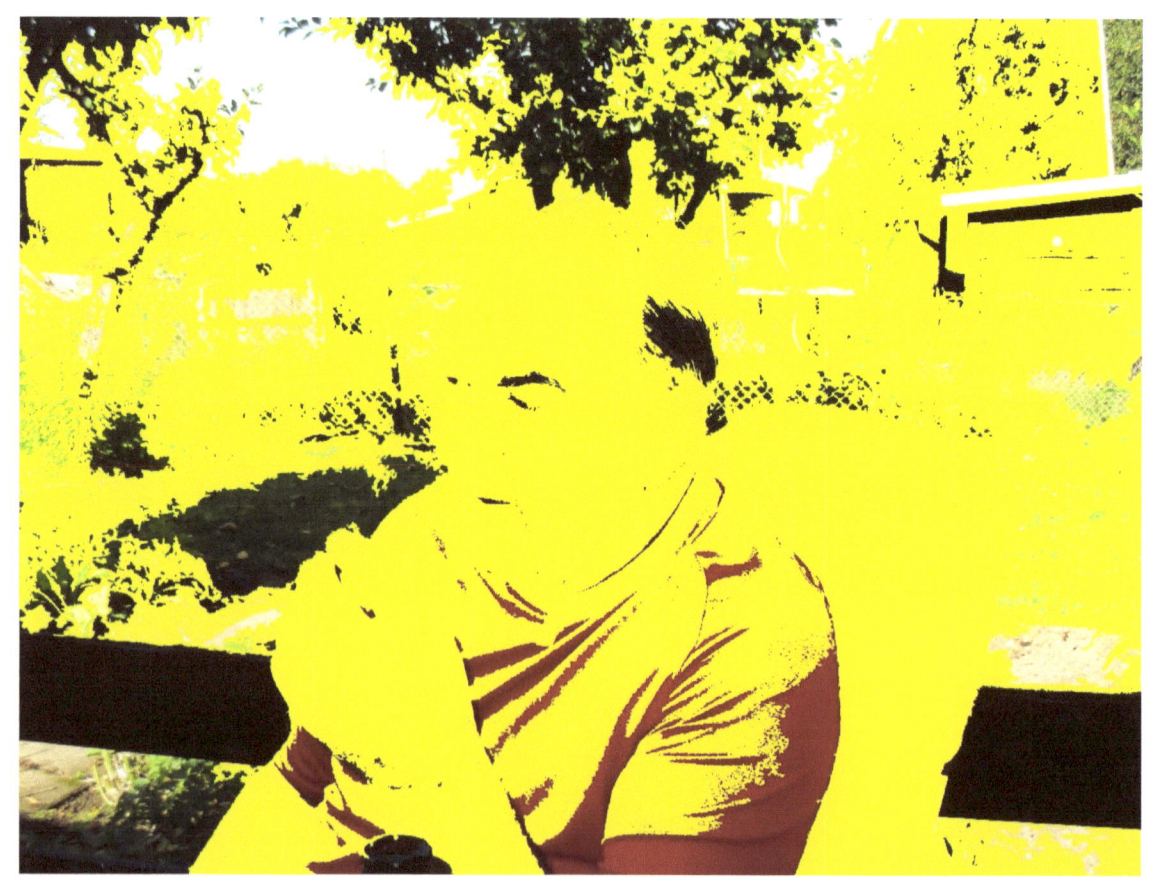

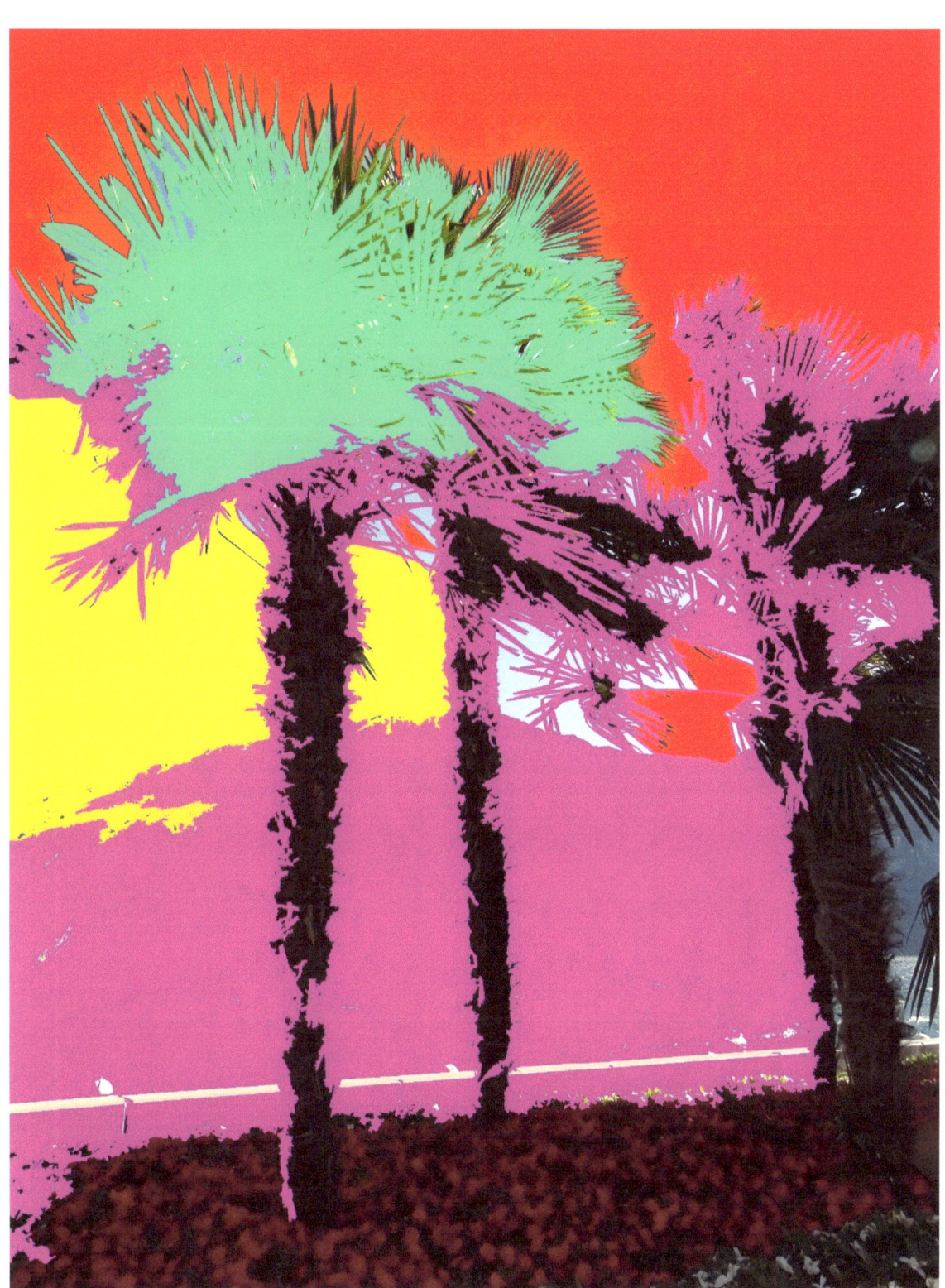

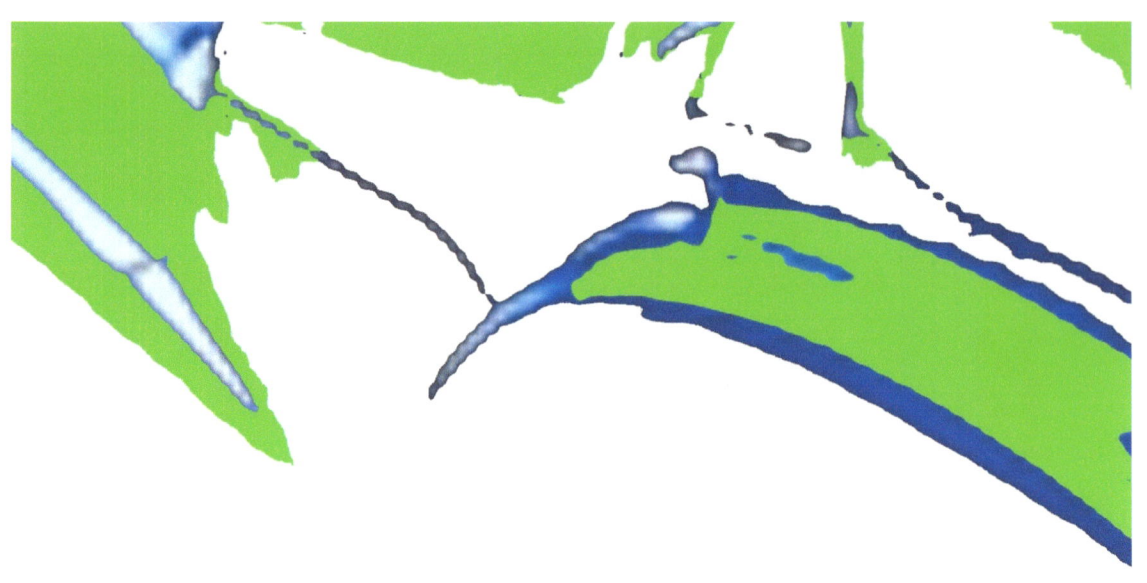
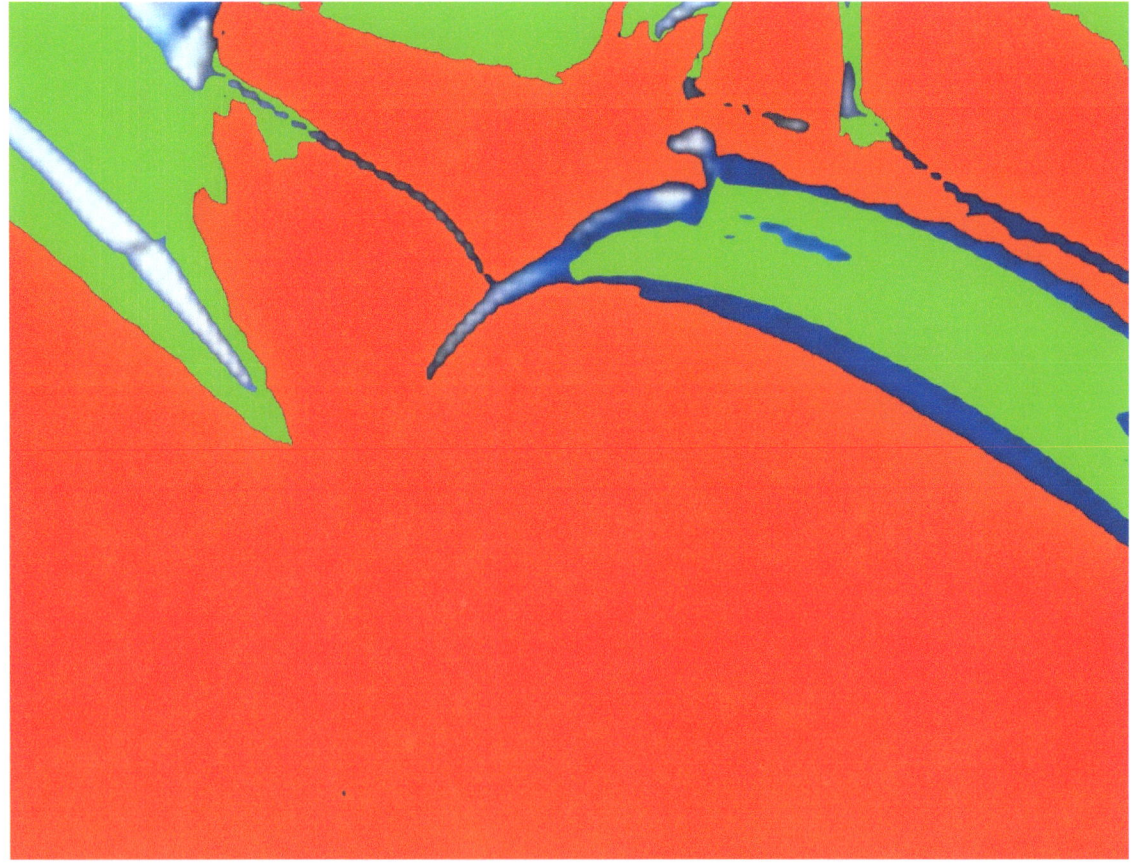

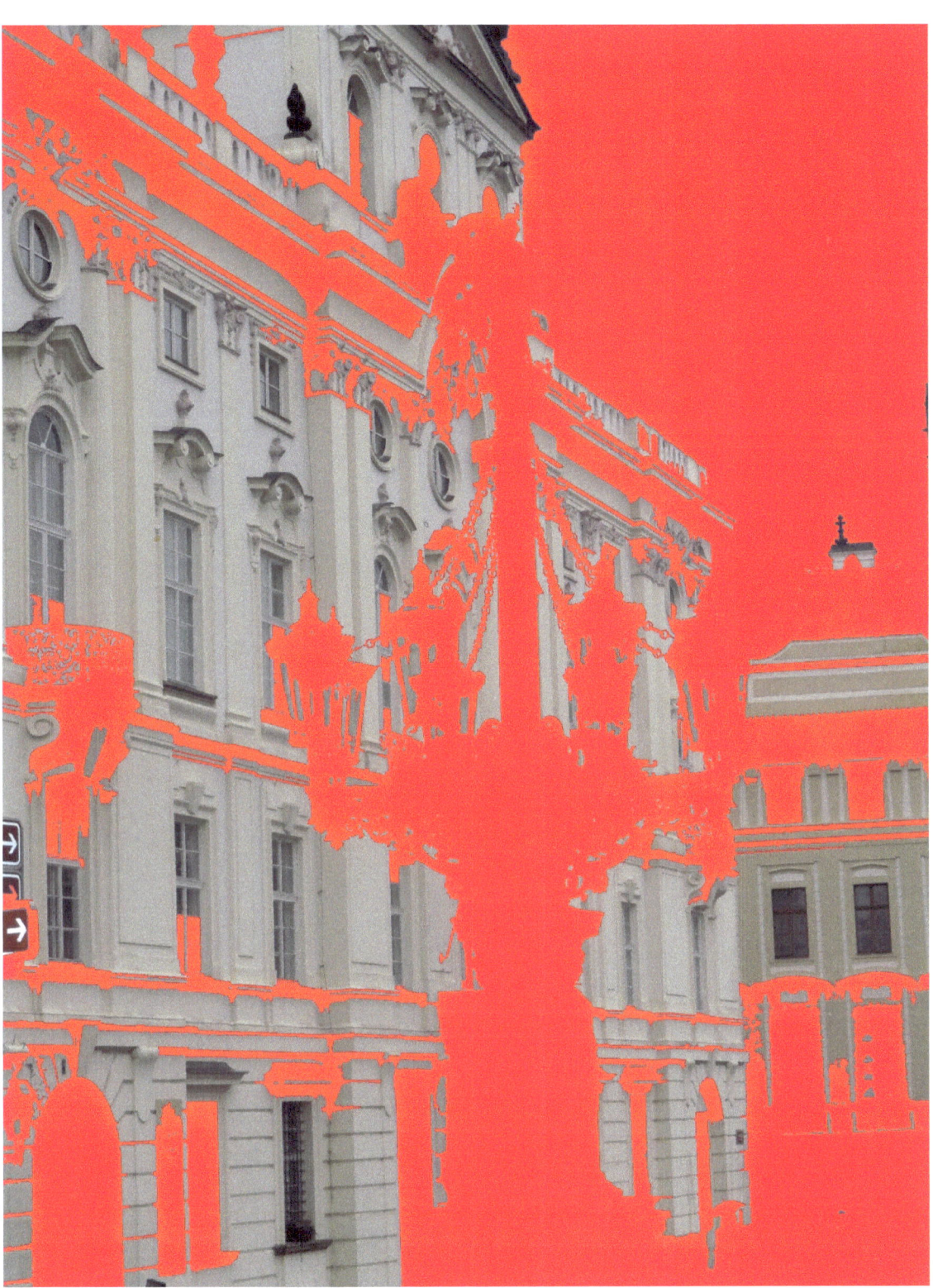

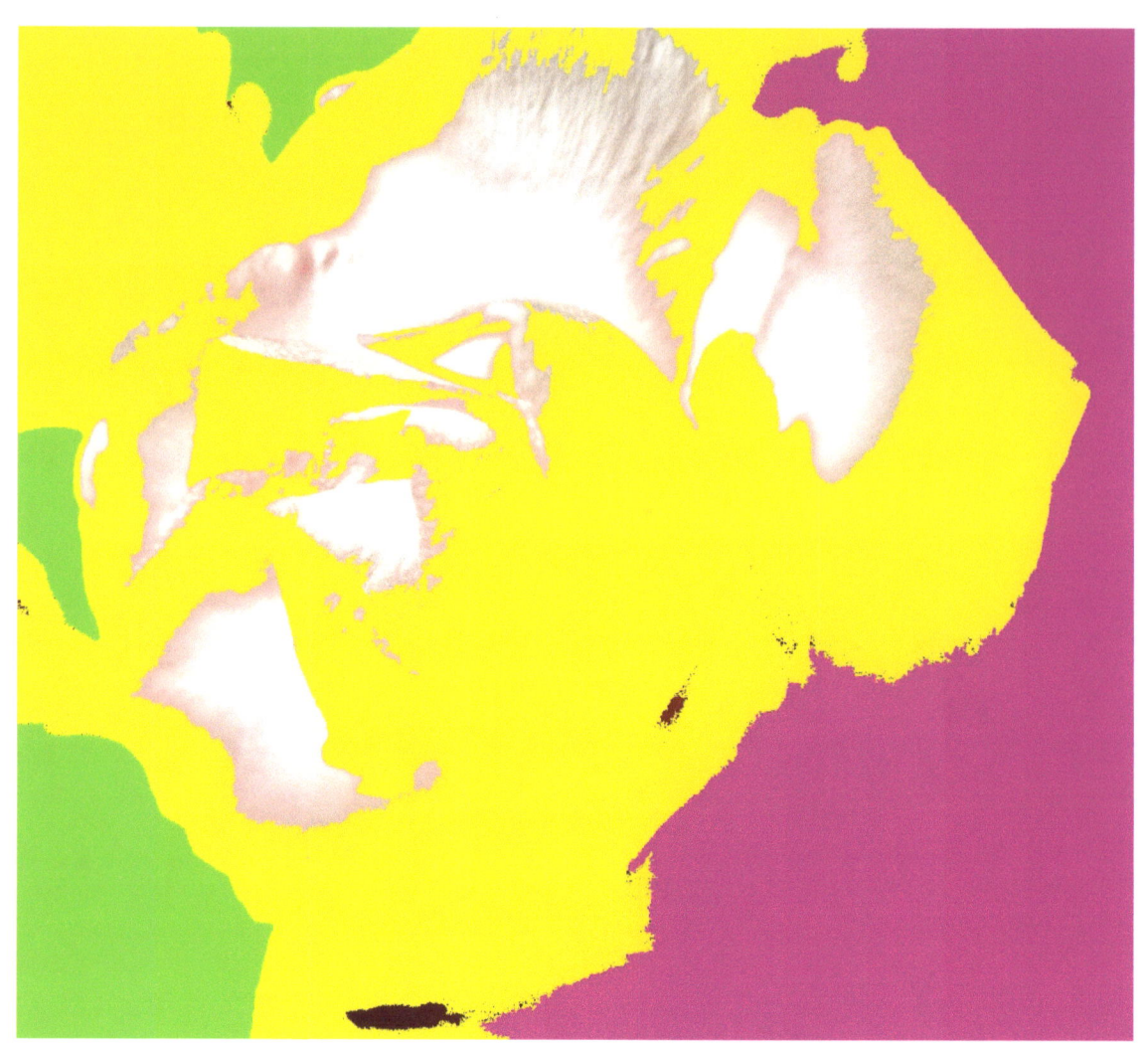

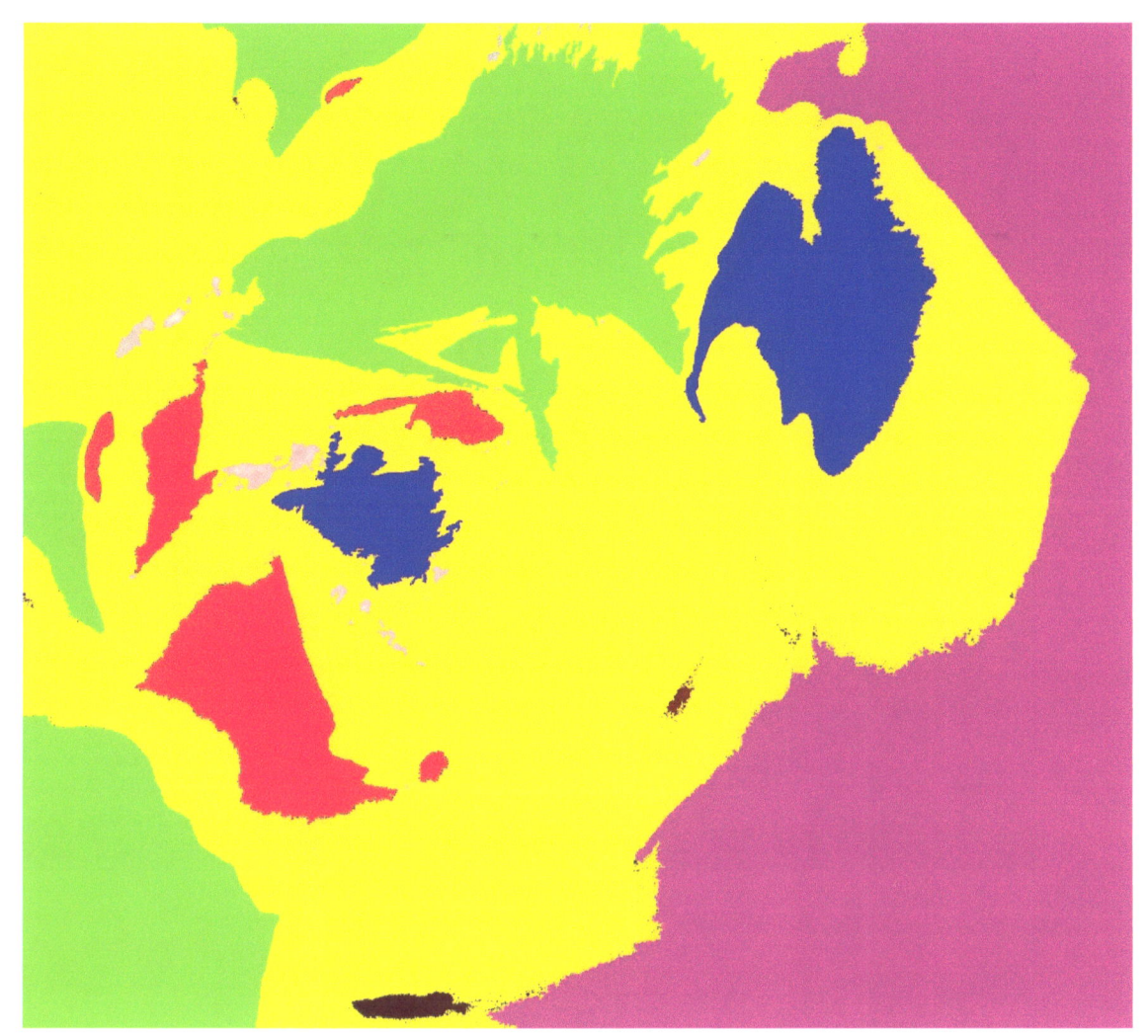

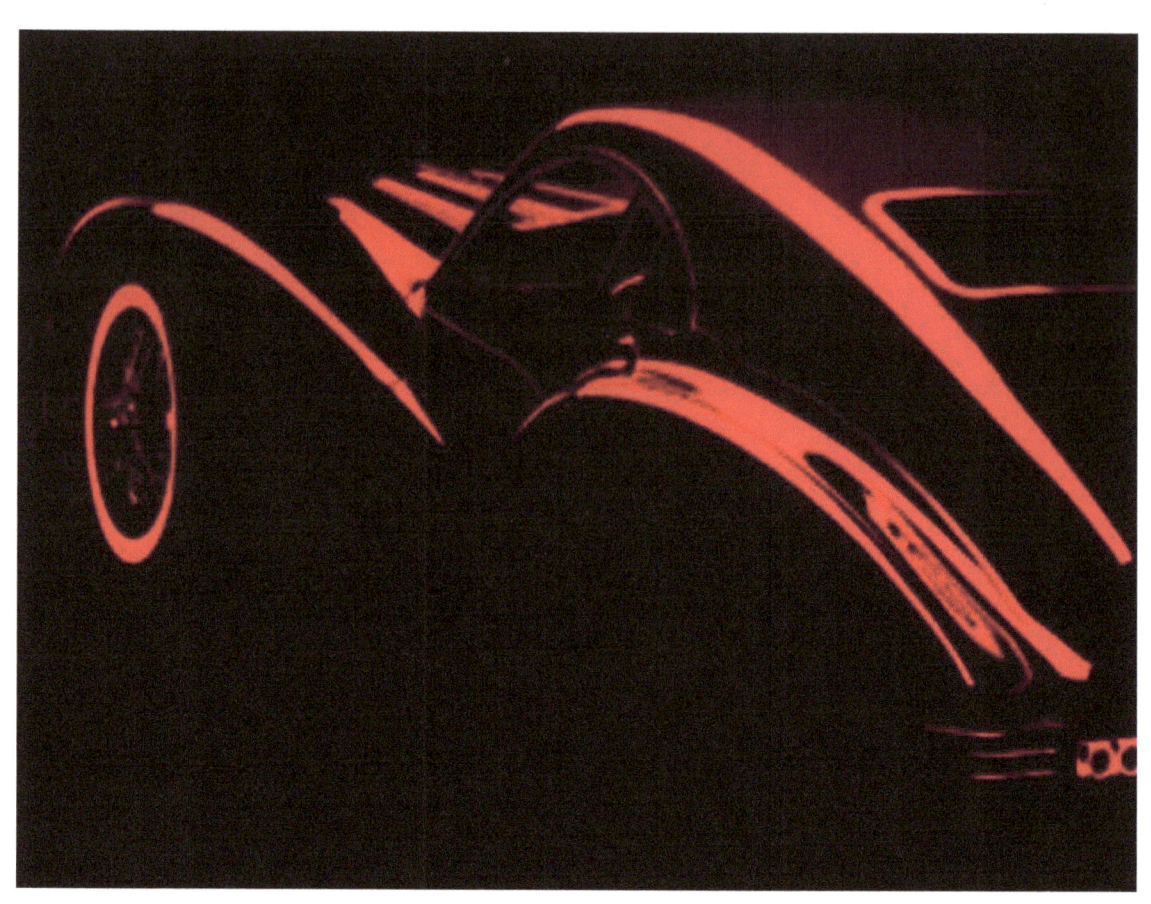
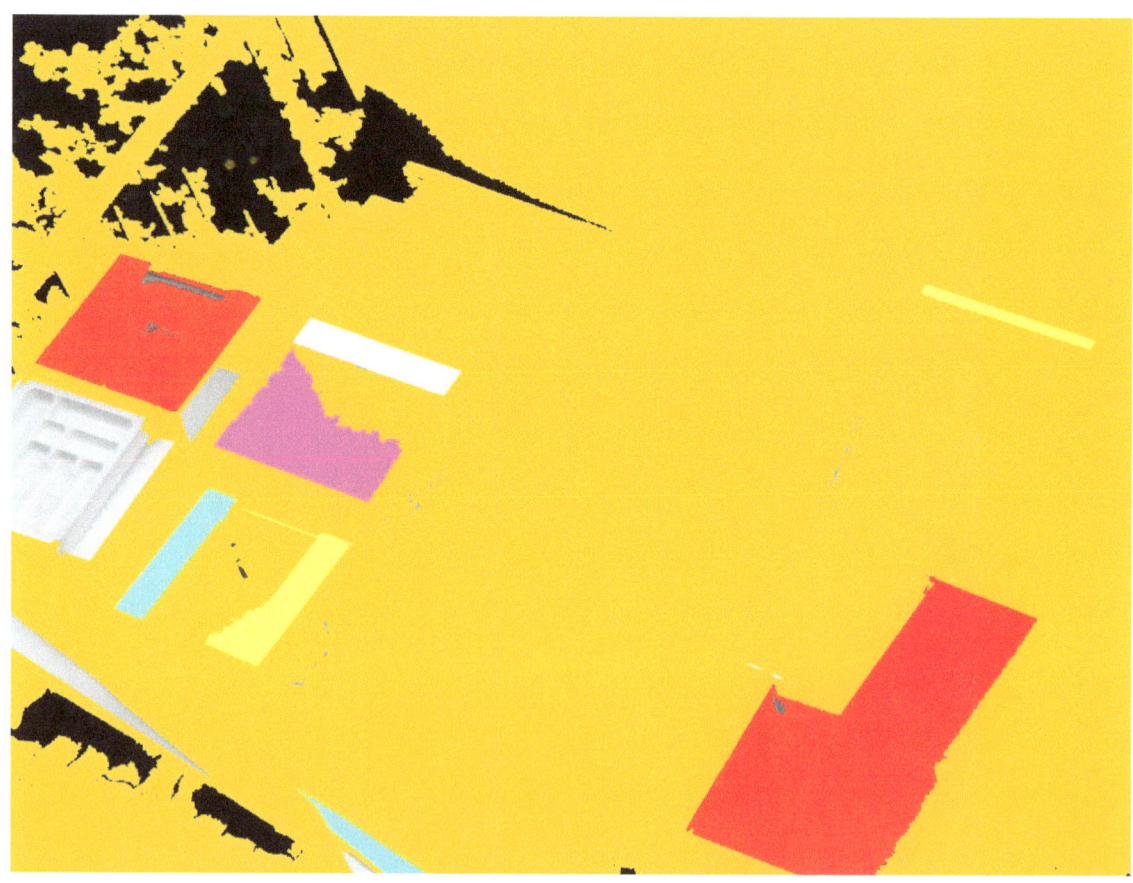

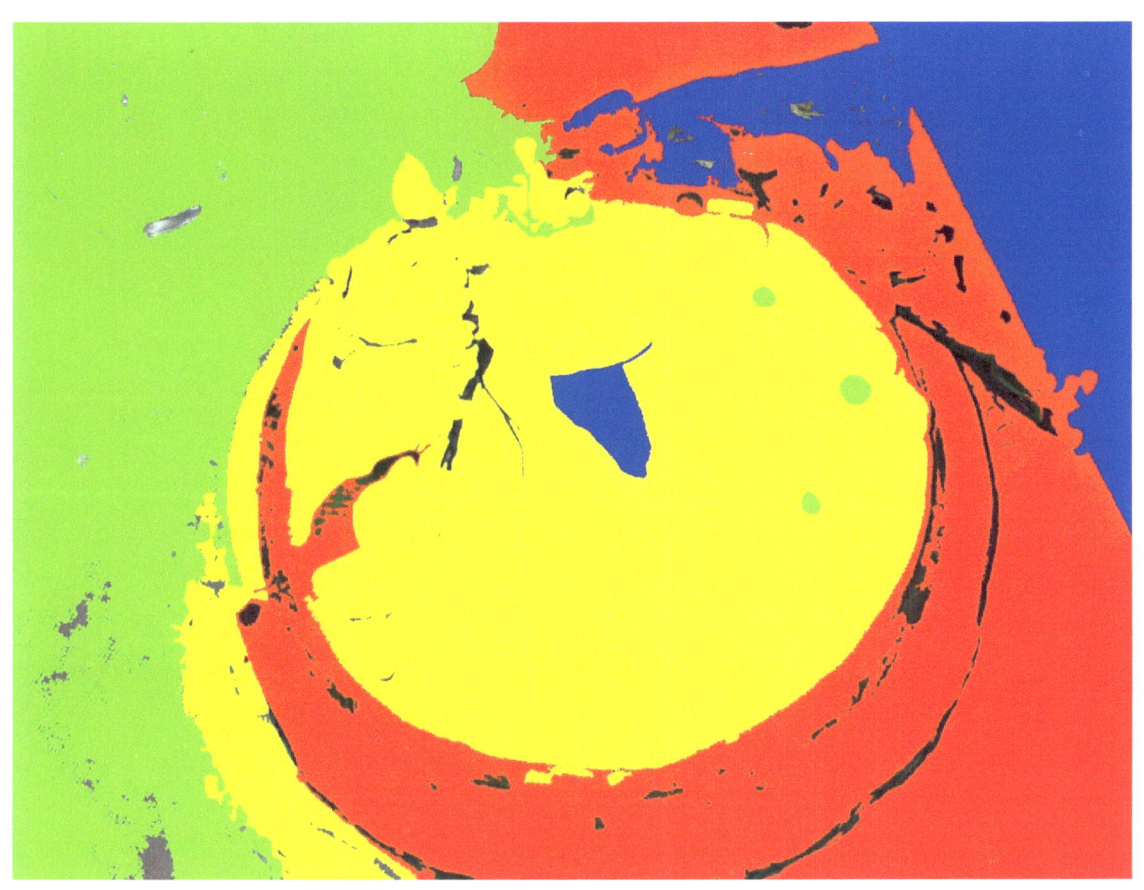
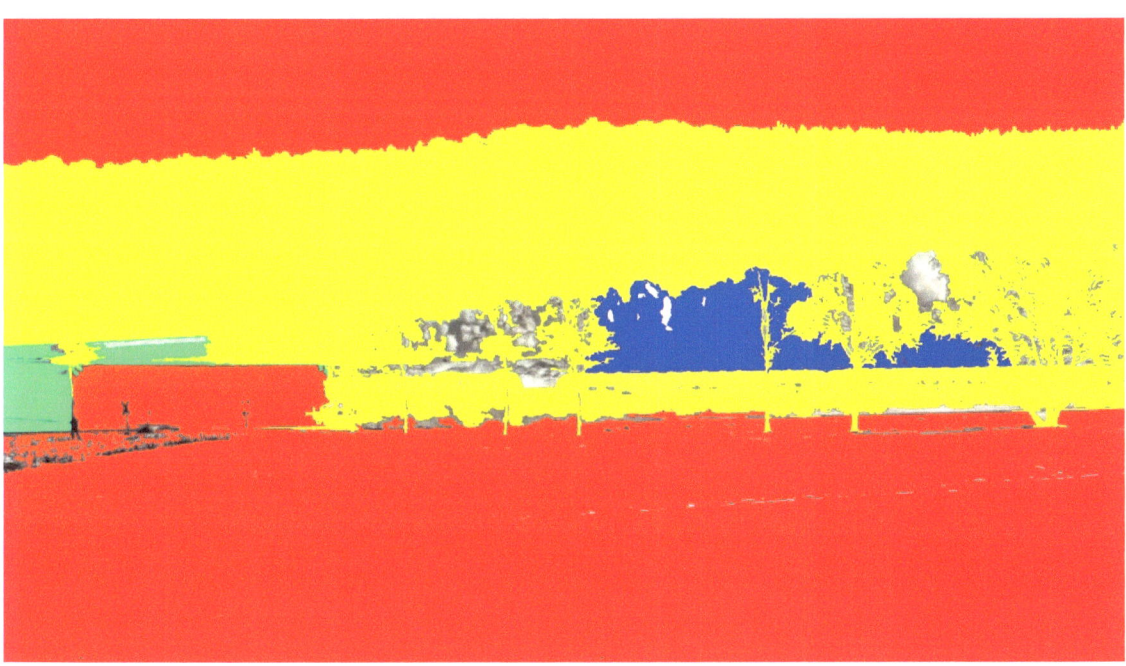

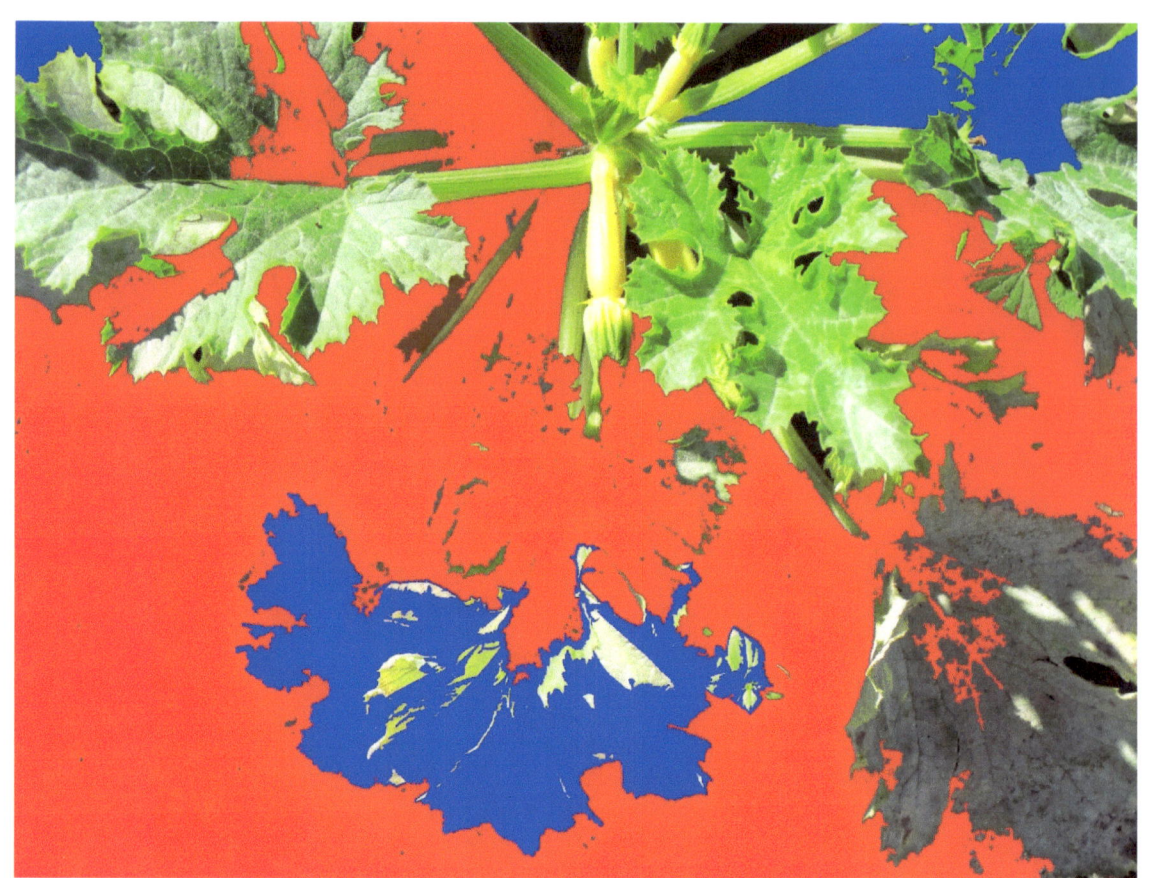

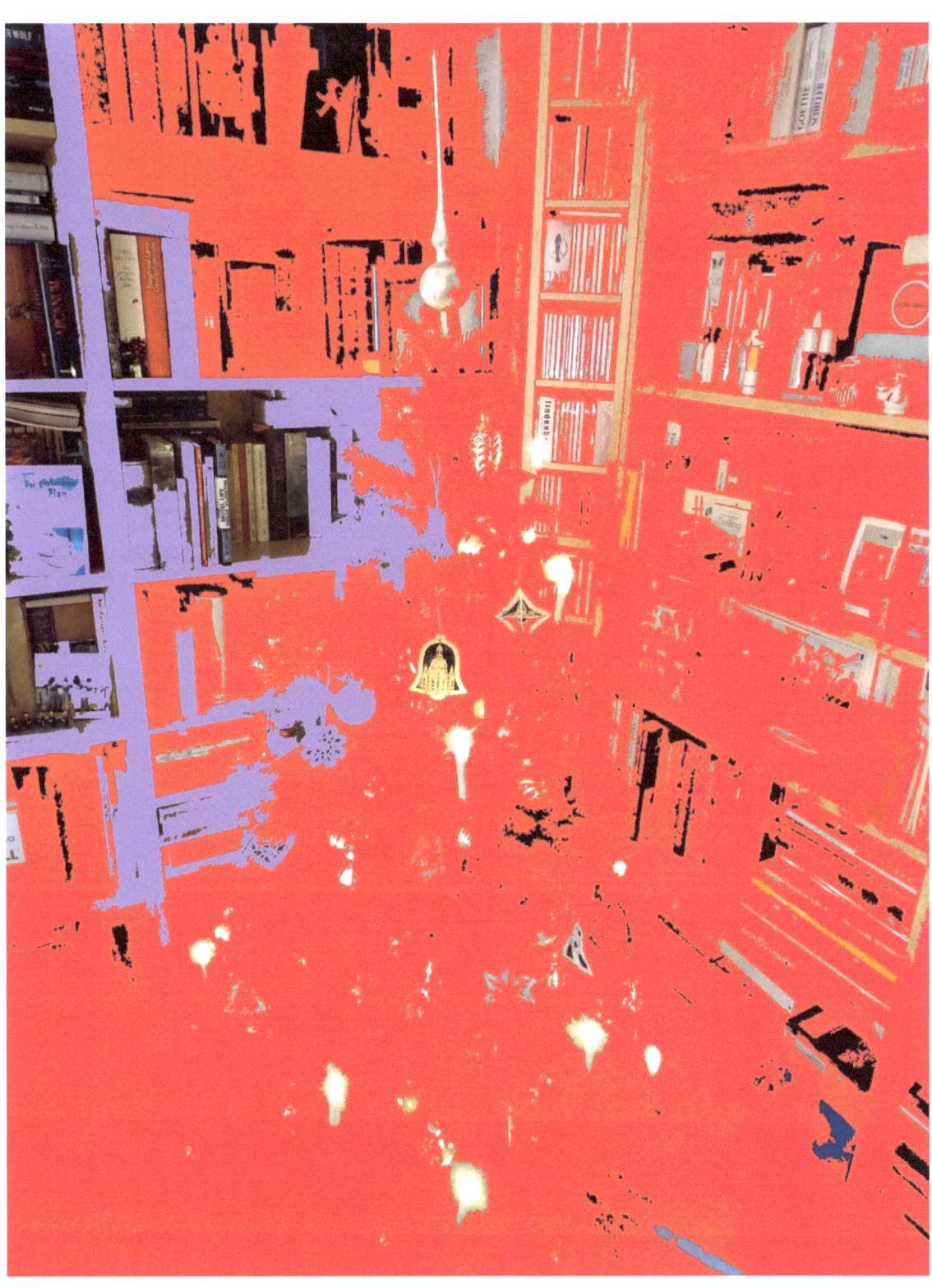

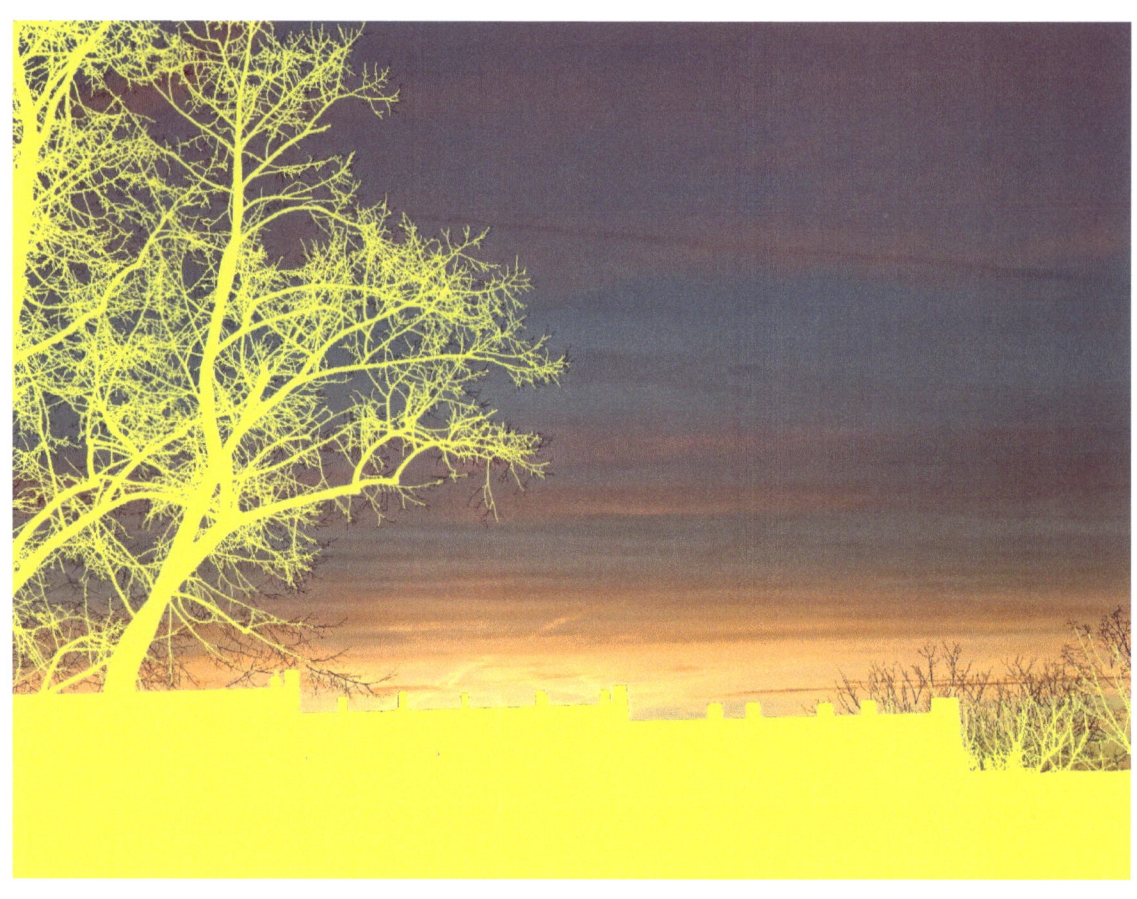
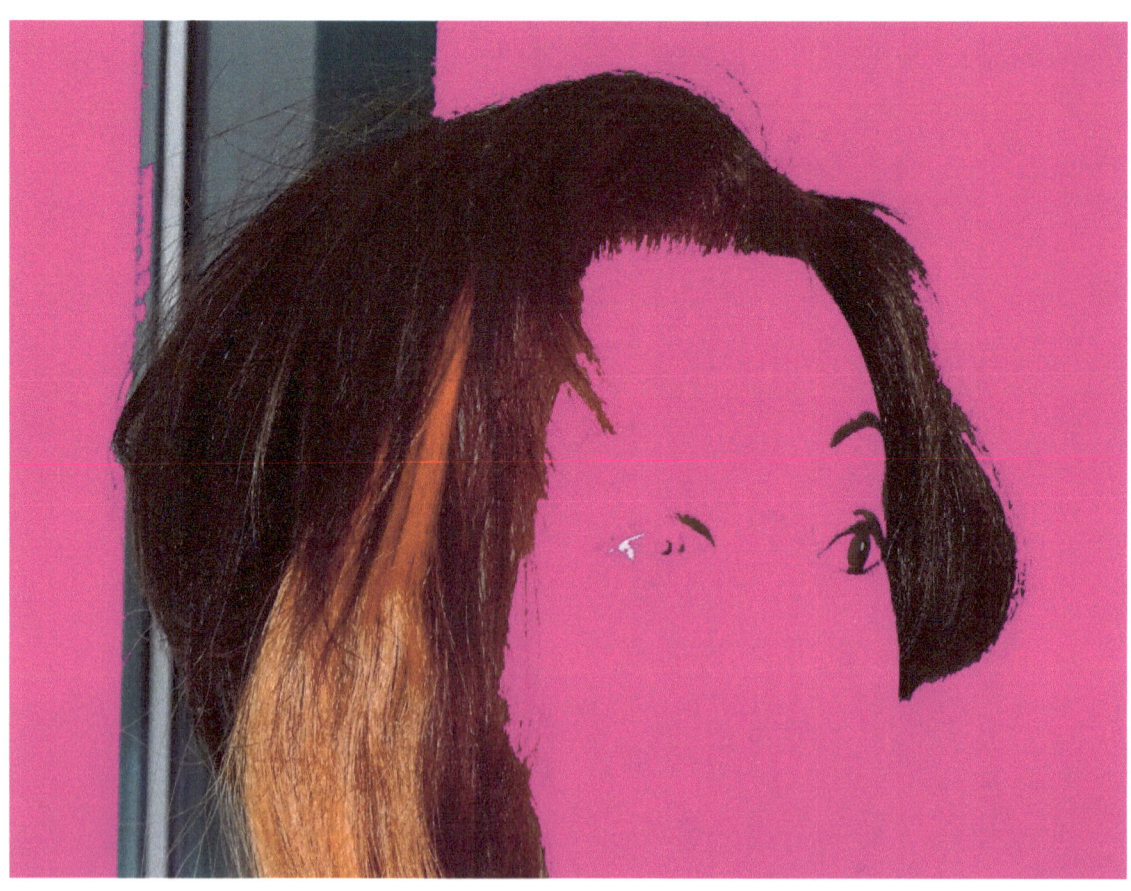

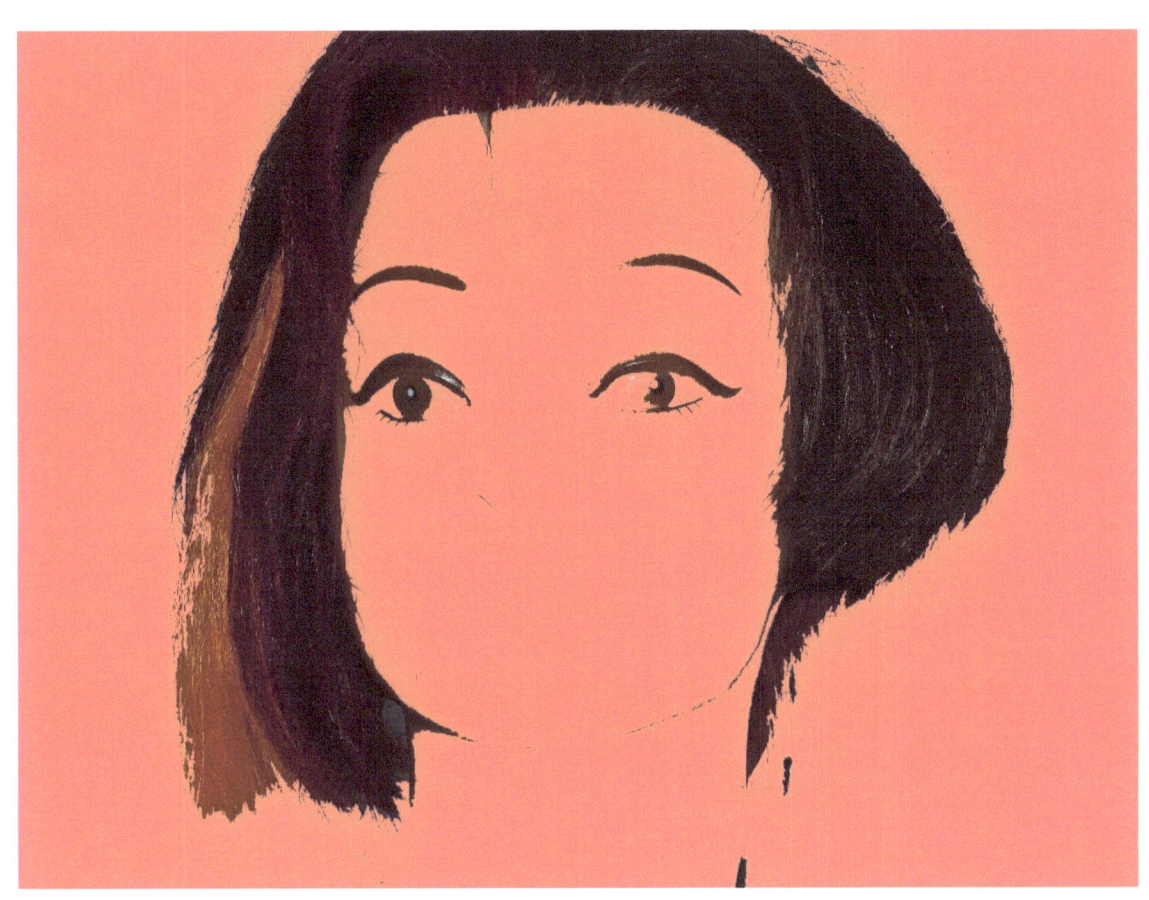

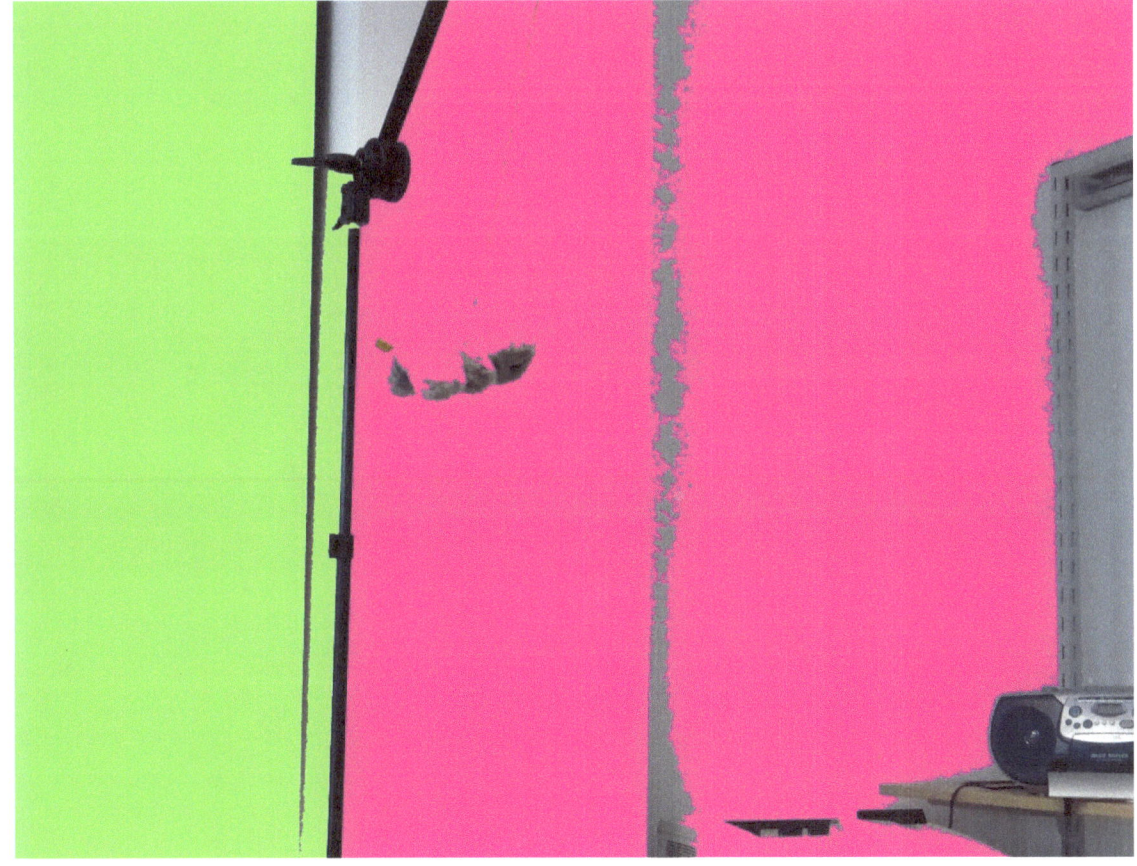

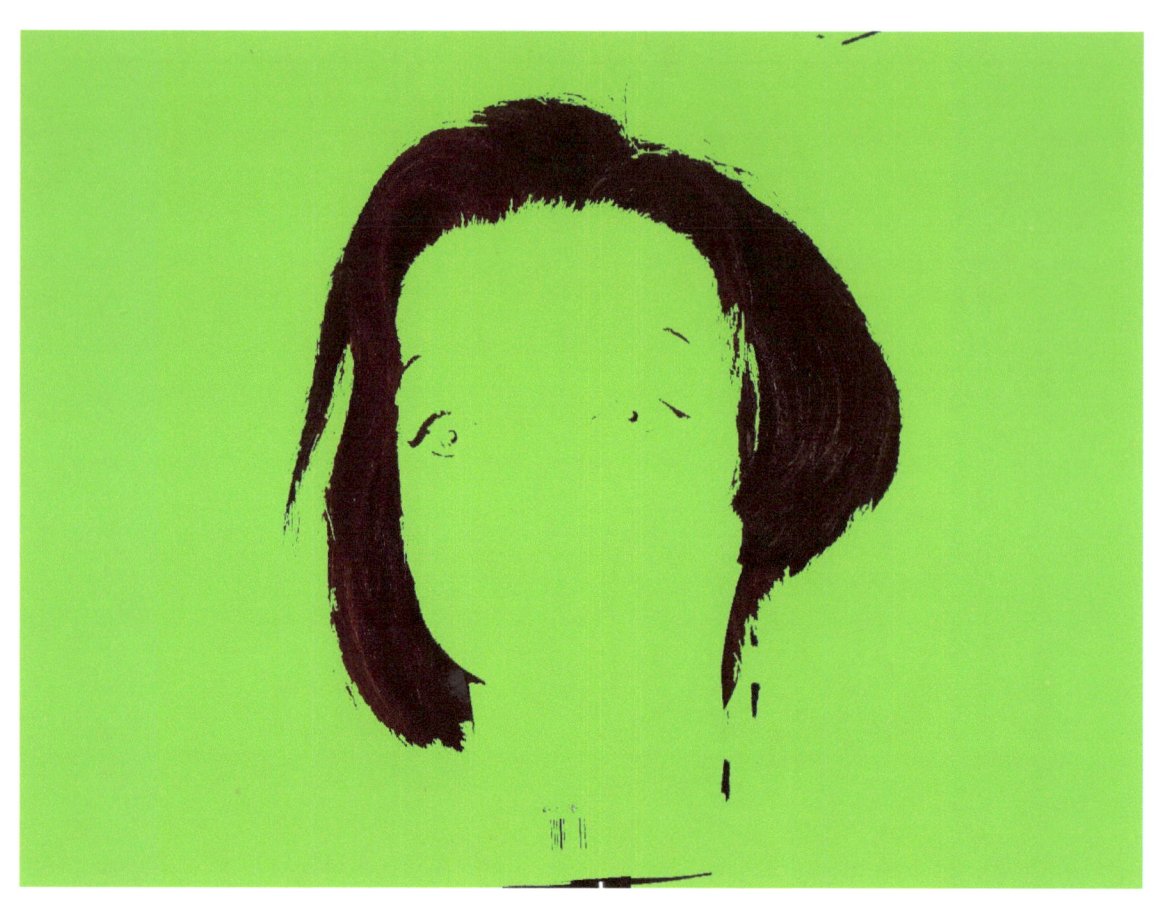
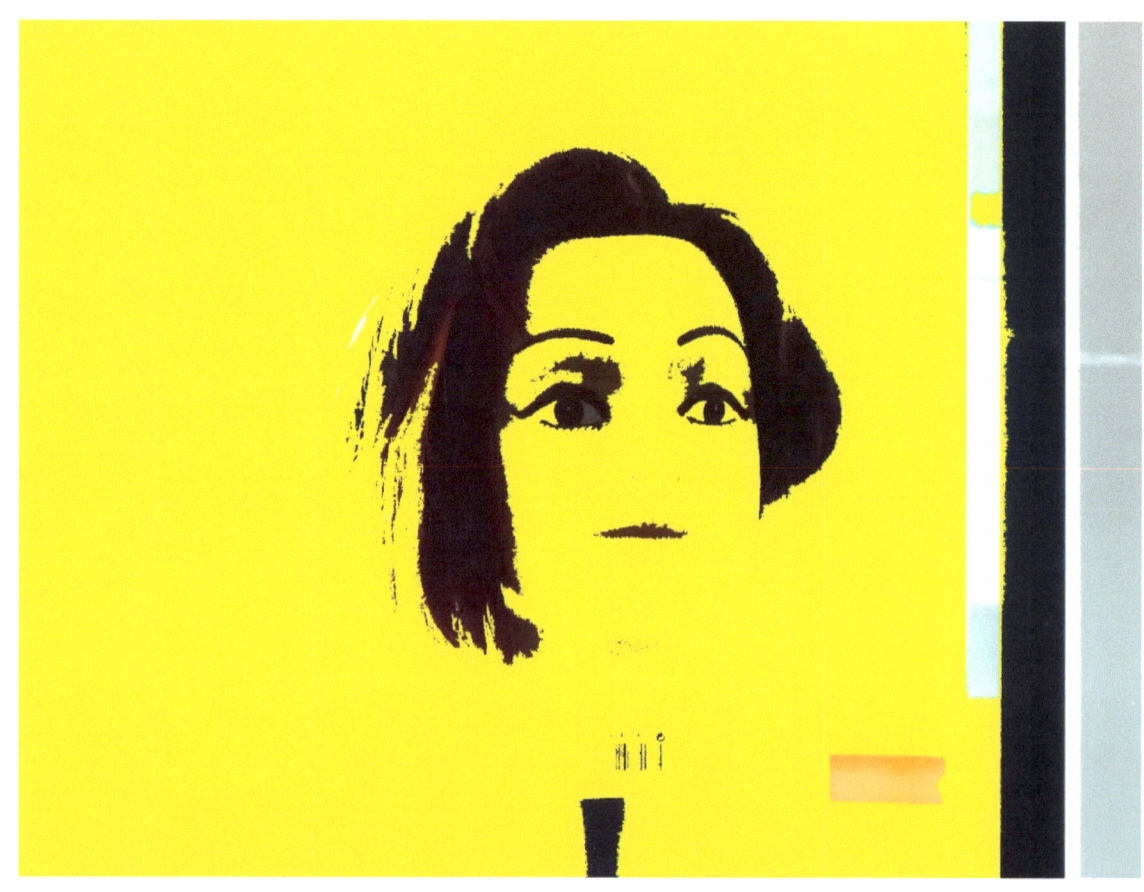

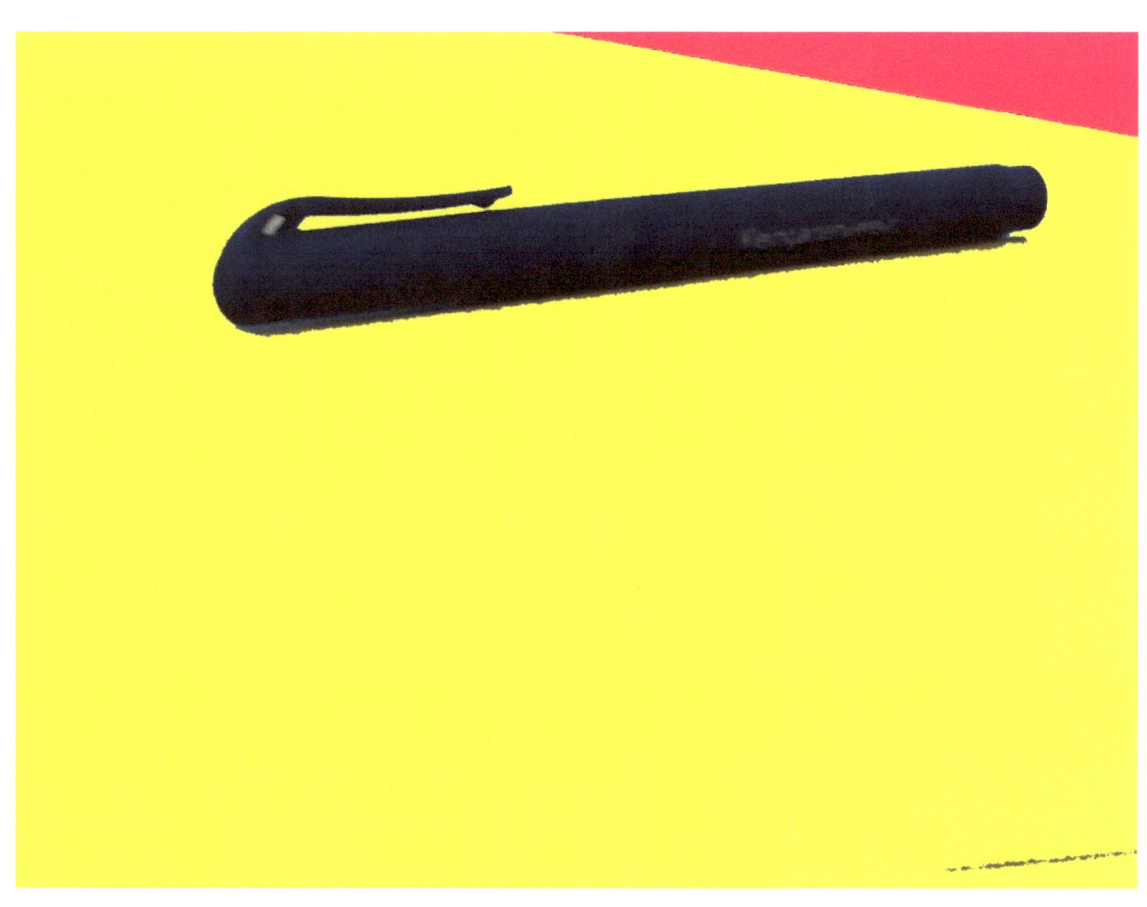

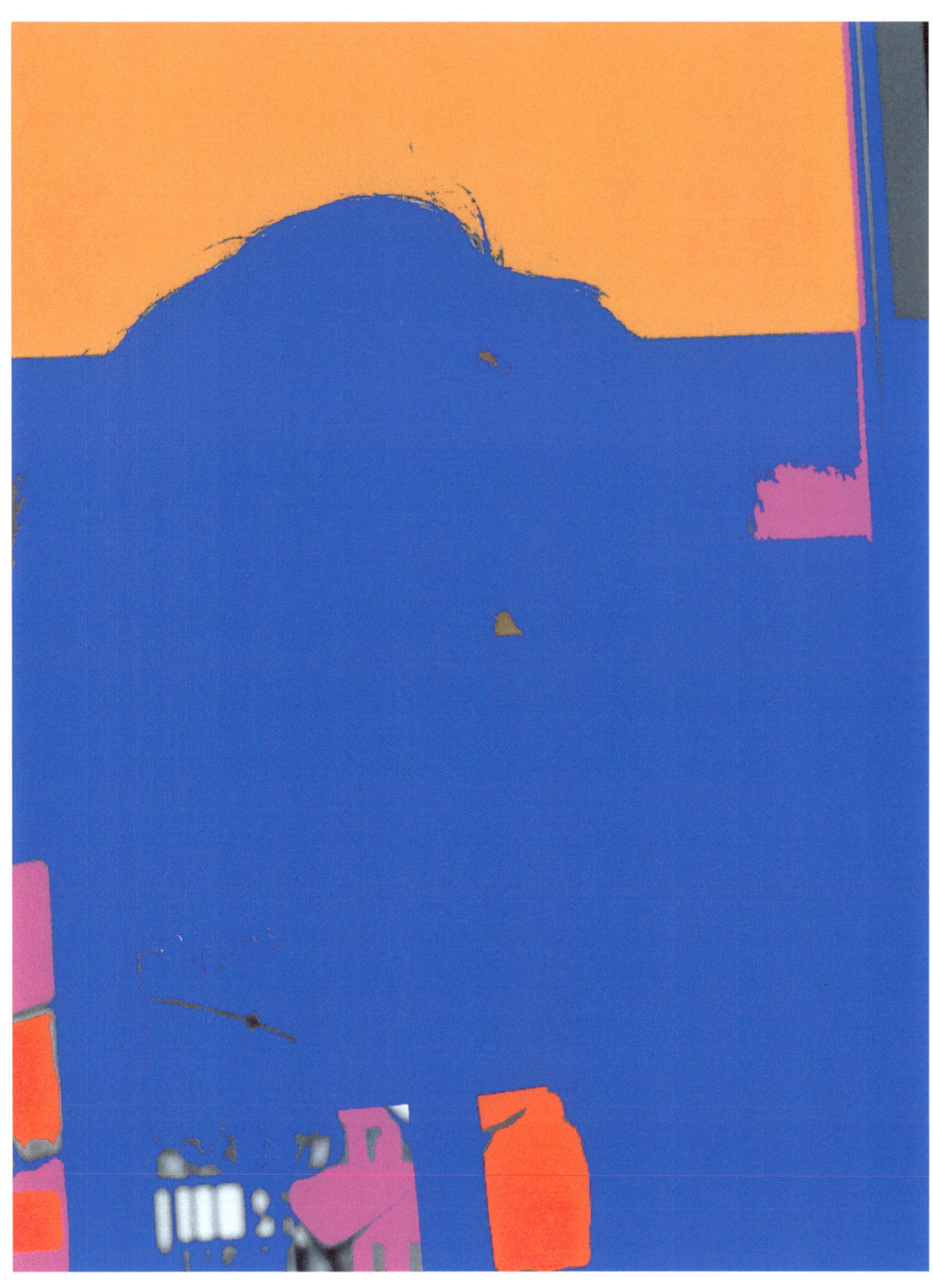

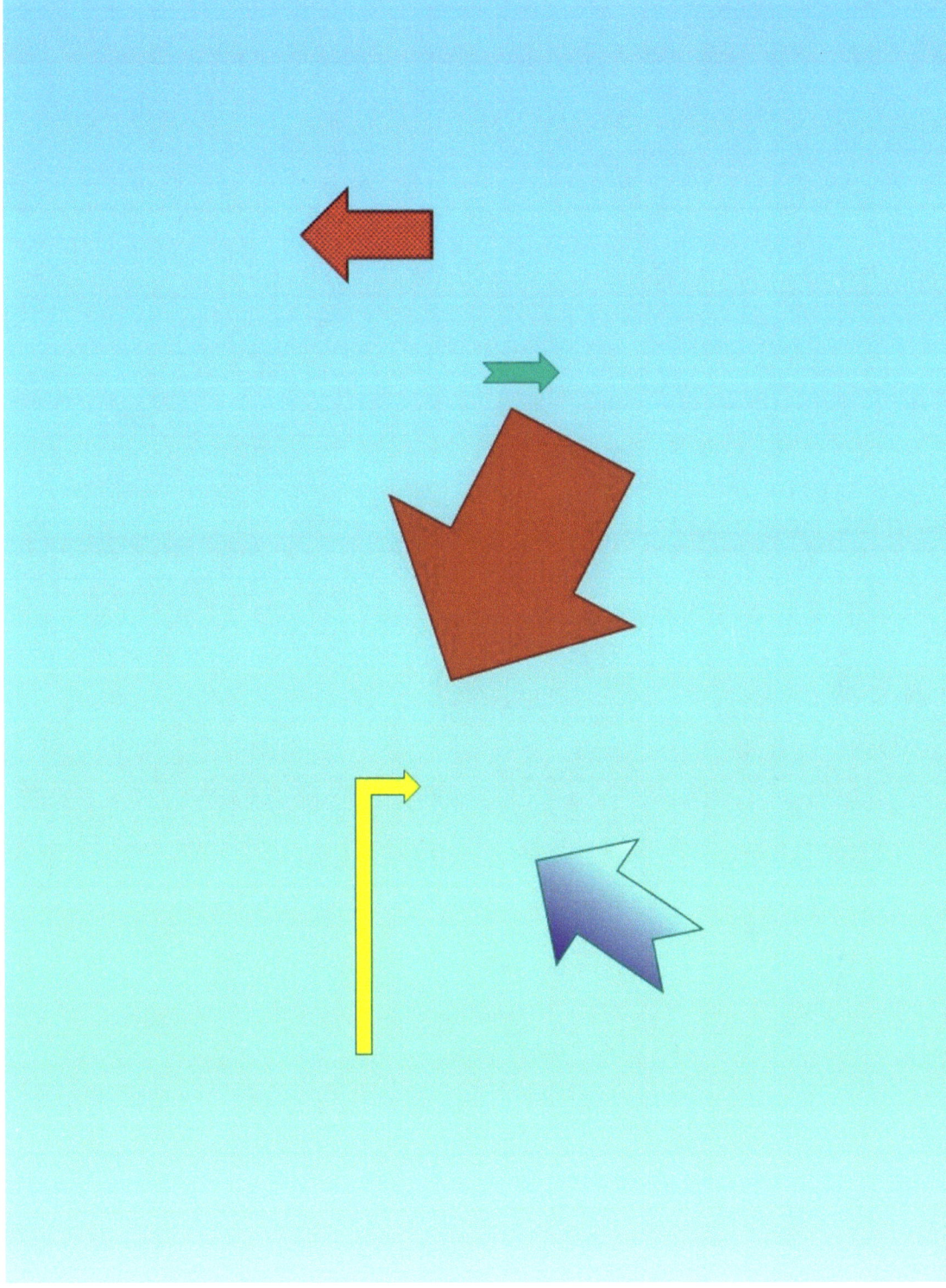

www.ingramcontent.com/pod-product-compliance
Lightning Source LLC
Chambersburg PA
CBHW040452220526
45473CB00004B/1606